On
Giants'
Shoulders

My dear Lucy,
I wrote this book for you, as from one generation to the next. Of course you are too young for it now, but maybe some day you can take it down from some upper shelf, dust it, and tell me what you think of it. And if you never do, just remember what they say in Geneva:
Post tenebras, LUX!

For related resources, visit
www.great-theologians.org

Michael Reeves

On Giants' Shoulders

•• Introducing great theologians ••
From Luther to Barth

Inter-Varsity Press
Norton Street, Nottingham NG7 3HR, England
Email: ivp@ivpbooks.com
Website: www.ivpbooks.com

© Michael Reeves, 2011

First published 2011

British Library Cataloguing in Publication Data
A catalogue record for this book is available from the British Library.

ISBN: 978-1-84474-495-4

Set in Garamond 11/13pt
Typeset in Great Britain by Servis Filmsetting Ltd, Stockport, Cheshire
Printed and bound in Great Britain by Ashford Colour Press Ltd, Gosport,
Hampshire

*Inter-Varsity Press publishes Christian books that are true to the Bible and that communicate
the gospel, develop discipleship and strengthen the church for its mission in the world.*

*Inter-Varsity Press is closely linked with the Universities and Colleges Christian Fellowship,
a student movement connecting Christian Unions in universities and colleges throughout Great
Britain, and a member movement of the International Fellowship of Evangelical Students.
Website: www.uccf.org.uk.*

CONTENTS

ACKNOWLEDGMENTS

Having written such a very unoriginal book, I have a lot of people to thank. In fact, I feel I really ought to thank these theologians I am introducing, given how much I have learnt from them over the years. And then there are all the staff of the Universities and Colleges Christian Fellowship, who have borne with far too much bleating from me. They can blame the Director, Richard Cunningham. I, however, am profoundly grateful to him for that rare willingness of his to follow through on the conviction that theology really can enhance mission.

I also want to thank Dr Philip Duce at Inter-Varsity Press, who always makes publishing such a pleasure; Professor Carl Trueman, Dr Steve Holmes, Dr Steve Nichols and Professor Ron Frost for their kind attempts to improve the manuscript; Dr Domenico Giordano, for his warm assistance and clarification; and the late Professor Colin Gunton, who taught me so much about time-travel. Lucy and Mia made their own very special contribution: I think I am grateful for that. I certainly am for the TULIP boys, who are a constant encouragement – and, in fact, both wise and adept. But most of all I thank my wonderful wife, Bethan. It is not easy walking with dinosaurs, but she has done it with unending love and grace.

INTRODUCTION: SNOBS, BUMPKINS AND DINOSAURS

C. S. Lewis was a self-confessed dinosaur. He knew perfectly well that he simply did not belong in the modern world. Yet, being born out of due time, he was able to spot what the natives could not. And what he saw in modern culture, perhaps more than anything else, was a suffocating enslavement to the beautiful myth of progress, the dream that history is evolving ever onwards and upwards, that newer is better.

It is the sort of belief that sits very comfortably in the subconscious, giving one the warm glow of knowing that we are faster, better, wiser, more advanced and more knowledgeable than our parents and forebears. Yet one of the problems Lewis noticed in the myth was that such superiority tends to produce not wisdom but ignorance. If we assume that the past is inferior, we will not bother consulting it, and will thus find ourselves stranded on the tiny desert island of our moment in time. Or, as Lewis put it, we will become like the country bumpkin, full of

> the cocksure conviction of an ignorant adolescent that his own village (which is the only one he knows) is the hub of the universe and does

everything in the Only Right Way. For our own age, with all its accepted
ideas, stands to the vast extent of historical time much as one village
stands to the whole world.[1]

Of course, such 'chronological snobbery' does not like to admit
its own existence. No snob likes to be thought of as an ignorant
bumpkin. Indeed, the chronological snob will often be the first
to bedeck himself with historical references. The modern writer
will allude to the old. But so often it is simply a case of the living
plundering the dead. The cachet of the Augustine, the Luther, the
Aquinas is purloined, as sound bites from their writings are torn
from their original context and pressed into the service of other
arguments, or simply used as weapons in the latest theological
street fight.

But what Lewis found – and what reading old books makes very
clear – is that every age works with a large set of assumptions that
seem to it so self-evident they are never questioned. Like the pro-
verbial frog in the kettle, we find it almost impossible to get a real
sense of the water we inhabit, and can thus be blissfully unaware
of how faddish our beliefs are. It is very tempting for me now to
don the grand airs of a sage cultural critic and attempt to list what
our unquestioned assumptions are today. But anyone excavating
this book from the dusty bowels of some copyright library in fifty
years' time would only chuckle at the profound issues I had overlooked. They are simply part of the air we breathe every day, and
as such are quite invisible to us.

What to do? 'The only palliative', said Lewis, 'is to keep the
clean sea breeze of the centuries blowing through our minds.'[2]
That is, we refuse to imprison ourselves in the stuffy broom cup-
board of the present and safely familiar, and open up the doors to
the refreshing influences of other times. And practically?

---

1. C. S. Lewis, *Studies in Medieval and Renaissance Literature* (Cambridge:
   Cambridge University Press, 1966), p. 138.
2. C. S. Lewis, Introduction to *On the Incarnation* by Athanasius (London:
   Centenary, 1944; repr. Crestwood, N. Y.: SVS, 1998), p. 5.

It is a good rule, after reading a new book, never to allow yourself
another new one till you have read an old one in between. If that is too
much for you, you should at least read one old one to every three new
ones . . . Not, of course, that there is any magic about the past. People
were no cleverer then than they are now; they made as many mistakes
as we. But not the *same* mistakes. They will not flatter us in the errors
we are already committing; and their own errors, being now open and
palpable, will not endanger us. Two heads are better than one, not
because either is infallible, but because they are unlikely to go wrong in
the same direction. To be sure, the books of the future would be just as
good a corrective as the books of the past, but unfortunately we cannot
get at them.[3]

Such is the motivation behind *On Giants' Shoulders* and its preceding companion volume *The Breeze of the Centuries*. It is that, far
from turning us into *irrelevant* dinosaurs, reading old books can
rescue us from bumpkinery and enlarge our vision. From other
centuries we receive an enrichment we could never have through
mere feeding on ourselves. And if that is true for old books in
general, it is more so for the books of old theologians. Theology is
something to be done corporately, by the church. But if we ignore
what the bulk of the church has said down through history, then
we act as schismatically as if we ignored the church on earth today.
More so, in fact.

Would Lewis not be appalled?

Clearly, then, this is a work built on Lewis's foundations. And yet,
is this not exactly the sort of dreary modern book Lewis feared
would insulate people from the health-giving breeze? Why write
another new book when the aim is to have people read old ones?

But this was just why Lewis wrote so much. The fact is,
theologians like Athanasius and Calvin are like famous guests of
honour at a party. Most people there would love to have some

---

3. Ibid. pp. 4–5.

time with them, but few dare to approach them without a polite introduction. And providing a few introductions to fascinating but potentially intimidating celebrity theologians is the aim of these pages.

In that sense, while there might seem to be an insane arrogance to the thought of trying to squeeze such titans into so few pages, this is actually a work that makes no great pretences. Rather, it seeks to do itself out of a job by leading readers on to better books than this. For that reason I will not spend time pontificating on 'Anselm's view of God' or 'Barth's view of Scripture' – to do so could leave readers just as frightened of approaching the great men for themselves, perhaps more so. Instead, I will try to intrude as little as possible, simply letting the reader get to know the theologians on their own terms. Of course that will not be entirely possible – and there will be moments when I will be unable to restrain myself from commenting – but that is the aim: not to pre-digest, pillage or spin, but to introduce real people, and that means people whose thoughts are so often a puzzling swirl of glories and gaffes.

Reading these introductions

Each introduction will begin with a little biography and background – after all, no theology is written in a vacuum, and somehow, knowing about, say, Athanasius' sense of humour and his 'Boy's Own' adventures makes Athanasius easier to get into. Then on to the theology, which will amount to a fast jog through each theologian's major work(s). Note: this is rather different from my writing on 'Calvin's doctrine of election' or the like; instead, I will try to walk with readers through Calvin's *Institutes*, getting to know its structure, feel and argument. Readers interested in Calvin's doctrine of election should then feel confident enough to put Reeves on one side and converse with Calvin direct. At the end of each introduction I will make some suggestions for getting to know that theologian better, and I will provide a timeline to help give a snapshot-sense of the order and context of the life in question.

There is a story that emerges from these pages, and readers who work through one introduction after another should, by the end of this second volume, have glimpsed something of the overall movement and flow of Christian thought through the centuries. However, this is just as much a work to dip in and out of. Its purpose is not so much to tell a grand narrative as to meet and get to know some of the key characters. And those characters are remarkably diverse: some will sound more winning, more trustworthy or more familiar; others may seem quite alien or off-putting. Thus if you find yourself floundering or overly enraged by one theologian, feel happy to move on to the next. He will, assuredly, be quite different.

But why these theologians, and not others? Quite simply, the goal of this work is to make accessible what otherwise seems intimidating, but if the very girth of the volumes was daunting, it would have failed in what it set out to do. I have therefore had to pick and choose theologians to introduce, and that means disappointing those whose heroes are not included. Still, I have not simply come up with a list of personal favourites; I have minor disagreements with every theologian here, and major problems with a few. Nor is this my list of 'great Christians'. Francis of Assisi, John Bunyan and John Wesley will make no appearance, though undoubtedly they were great and influential; it is that their greatness was not so much *as theologians*. Rather, I have tried to choose theologians who are influential or significant especially for the English-speaking world (many of whom, I suspect, are the very ones English-speaking people are most eager to know better). As a result, such mighty names as Origen, Palamas, Gerhard, Turretin and Suárez (the list could go on) are not included. My apologies to any who miss them: accessibility calls.

The last word of introduction really belongs to C. S. Lewis, who grasped so well the point of wrestling with theology:

> For my own part I tend to find the doctrinal books often more helpful in devotion than the devotional books, and I rather suspect that the same experience may await many others. I believe that many who find that 'nothing happens' when they sit down, or kneel down, to a book of devotion, would find that the heart sings unbidden while they are

working their way through a tough bit of theology with a pipe in their teeth and a pencil in their hand.[4]

May it be so for you now.

---

4. Ibid. p. 8.

1. THE WORD DID EVERYTHING

Martin Luther

Five hundred years after his extraordinary life, Martin Luther remains perhaps the most controversial theologian of all time. His piercing thought, uncompromising directness and often lavatorial offensiveness have made him as vilified by some as he is venerated by others. Yet the strength of his grasp on the sheer graciousness of God towards sinners, coupled with the originality and vigour of his expression, make him incomparably stimulating for anyone to read. Actually, 'stimulating' is hardly the word; reading Luther is like being slapped in the face. It hardly ever fails to leave one gasping.

The difficulty with Luther is that he never wrote a systematic presentation of his thought; he devoted his efforts instead to biblical commentaries, sermons and small treatises. The advantage is the easy accessibility of the short works; the disadvantage is that, because there are so many of them, it can be hard to grasp the overall shape of his theology. In order to get a toehold on him, we will focus on the crucial turns in his theological development, looking especially at his Heidelberg Disputation, and then leaf through the essential points of his mature thought as seen in his main Reformation treatises.

Luther's life

On 10 November 1483 Luther (or Luder as he then was) was born
in Eisleben in central Germany. Like most people in Eisleben, his
father was in the mining industry, but he had aspirations for his
son, and so, when he could, he sent him off to study law. Young
Martin, however, suffered more than most from a classic fear of
the age: that of sudden death. The worry was that, without the
chance to confess all your latest sins to a priest, you would fail to
die in a state of grace. Imagine, then, his terror when a summer
lightning bolt knocked him to the ground as he walked from
his parents' house to his university. 'Saint Anne, help me! I shall
become a monk!' he cried to his patron saint. A monk he thus
became, and yet that only served to intensify his spiritual anxiety
(or *Anfechtung* as called it, meaning 'conflict', 'assault' or 'temptation'). Conducting his first mass, for instance, he was terrified by
the thought of the holy majesty of God. He spent more and more
time obsessively confessing his sins to a superior, paranoid that he
would forget some and so fail to be completely absolved. It forced
him to start seeing sin as something deeper than a matter of particular lapses, as a total sickness. Through extreme asceticism he
sought to earn merit before God. On a visit to Rome this included
climbing the Scala Sancta on his knees, repeating the Lord's Prayer
for each step, and kissing it.[1] Yet at the top he began to doubt
whether it had been of any avail.

On his return to Germany he was transferred to the Augustinian
monastery in Wittenberg. His superior, Johann von Staupitz,
had suggested that he become a doctor of theology and lecture
on the Bible at the university there. At least in that way Luther
might find some consolation in the Scriptures. Wittenberg was
a fitting place for Luther to think about repentance and forgiveness, for its overlord, Frederick 'the Wise', Elector of Saxony,
had amassed there one of the largest collections of saints' relics.

---

1. The Scala Sancta was the staircase that Jesus had supposedly climbed to
   appear before Pilate, and that had subsequently been brought to Rome by
   the emperor Constantine's relic-obsessive mother.

It was believed that the saints, through their exceptional holiness, had earned a surplus of merit that the pope could confer on souls, both living and dead, to alleviate the time they must spend in purgatory, the place where they must be purged and fitted for heaven. And, since the necessary merit came from the saints, it seemed appropriate to offer it to those who venerated their relics.

One of these papal 'indulgences' or gifts of merit was to be offered in the Castle Church of Wittenberg on 1 November (All Saints' Day) 1517 in return for a fee that would be used to build the new basilica of St Peter in Rome. Such offers were commonplace, but the issue of indulgences had recently been given special prominence by the antics of a travelling indulgence-monger, Johann Tetzel. Using crude emotional blackmail, he advertised the indulgences with such jingles as 'As soon as the coin in the coffer rings, / the soul from purgatory springs,' and 'Place your penny on the drum, / the pearly gates open and in strolls mum.'

In a pre-emptive strike, on 31 October, All Saints' Eve, Luther posted on the church door a summons to an academic disputation on the issue, consisting of ninety-five theses for debate. In it he asked questions such as why the pope did not release all souls from purgatory out of love, instead of charging for it. But at the heart of his criticism was the fact that the practice of indulgences effectively replaced the need for true repentance of the heart with a mere external transaction. Supporting this argument, he soon found that the proof-text used to validate the sacrament of penance from the Latin Vulgate was a mistranslation of the original Greek. In the Vulgate, Matthew 4:17 reads *penitentiam agite* (do penance), whereas the Greek meant 'change your mind', something internal and not merely external.

He could never have predicted the consequences of his action, but popular local grievance at German money being taken to Italy fuelled support for his critique. Meanwhile, his subsequent debates with church officials soon made it clear that the real issue was one of authority. Which had the final say: Bible or pope? In all this, though, Luther had not yet formulated his mature doctrine of justification by faith alone. That would come only in his 1519 'tower experience' (so named because he had his study in the monastery tower).[2] Then, studying Romans 1:17,

> I began to understand that the righteousness of God is that by which the righteous lives by a gift of God, namely by faith. And this is the meaning: the righteousness of God is revealed by the gospel, namely, the passive righteousness with which the merciful God justifies us by faith, as it is written, 'He who through faith is righteous shall live.' Here I felt that I was altogether born again and had entered paradise itself through open gates.[3]

With this, Luther's confidence in his stand against Rome grew dramatically. In late 1519 he declared that the pope was antichrist, and events began to move swiftly. In 1520 Pope Leo X issued a bull excommunicating Luther. Luther then publicly burned the bull along with the papal constitutions and books of scholastic theology, writing a counter-blast entitled *Against the Execrable Bull of Antichrist.* That same year he also wrote his key Reformation tracts *Treatise on Good Works, To the Christian Nobility of the German Nation, The Babylonian Captivity of the Church* and *The Freedom of a Christian.*

Luther now had the Holy Roman Emperor (Charles V), the pope, a number of high-ranking churchmen and seemingly a thousand years of church history against him. The following year he was summoned to a session (or 'diet') of the imperial court

---

2. There is a debate among Luther scholars as to precisely when Luther had his 'tower experience' and discovered the true meaning of the righteousness of God. Because he does talk about justification by faith early on, some believe his experience happened as soon as 1513, thus making the ninety-five theses a product of his new theology. Others hold that it was not until 1519, meaning that the ninety-five theses and his other early lectures pre-date his mature understanding of justification by faith. Luther himself clearly placed it in 1519, and I have followed his dating here.

3. 'Preface to the Complete Edition of Luther's Latin Writings', *Luther's Works*, ed. J. Pelikan (vols. 1–30, St. Louis: Concordia; vols. 31–55, Philadelphia: Fortress, 1955–76), vol. 34, pp. 336–337.

in Worms, where most assumed he would soon be burned for heresy. When he arrived he was initially so intimidated by the questioning in the presence of all the princes that he could hardly speak. The papal nuncio took Luther to be too stupid to have written all that he had, and wanted to know who really was behind the Reformation tracts. Then, after an order to recant, came Luther's final answer:

> I am bound by the Scriptures I have quoted and my conscience is captive to the Word of God. I cannot and I will not retract anything, since it is neither safe nor right to go against conscience. I cannot do otherwise, here I stand, may God help me, Amen.[4]

Luther was condemned to death as a heretic. But he had already disappeared.

What had happened was that his prince, Frederick 'the Wise' of Saxony, had decided to hide him. He arranged for armed horsemen to kidnap Luther and take him to the Wartburg Castle where he remained, in disguise, for nearly a year. In that time he translated the entire New Testament from its original Greek into German. For the first time in a millennium the people would be able to read a reliable version of the Scriptures for themselves. Thus Luther repaid Rome in kind, sounding the death-knell to all its power.

Unfortunately, during his time in hiding, trouble was brewing in Wittenberg. Church practice was being reformed at a rate that the people were unable to cope with. Also, three men from Zwickau arrived, claiming to be prophets who had no need of the Bible since the Lord spoke to them directly; they repudiated infant baptism and advocated the speeding of the kingdom of God through the slaughter of the ungodly. Wittenberg was spiralling into chaos, and Luther found himself facing a new opposition: the 'fanatics' of the radical Reformation.

Luther returned with a call for more careful reform:

---

4. 'Luther at the Diet of Worms', ibid. vol. 32, p. 112.

I will constrain no man by force, for faith must come freely without
compulsion. Take myself as an example. I opposed indulgences and
all the papists, but never with force. I simply taught, preached, and
wrote God's Word; otherwise I did nothing. And while I slept, or drank
Wittenberg beer with my friends Philip and Amsdorf, the Word so
greatly weakened the papacy that no prince or emperor ever inflicted
such losses upon it. I did nothing; the Word did everything.[5]

He also reacted strongly to the radicals, who, he believed, had mis-
taken the point of the Reformation: where he was revolting against
the spiritual pretensions of sinners, they were tilting at the external
things of the faith, such as the Bible and the sacraments. He saw in
their theology a new anti-external legalism.

In 1525 the ex-monk married an escaped nun, Katharina von
Bora, and proceeded to have five children with her. Together they
converted Luther's old Augustinian cloister into a family home
that became something of a model for the Protestant minister's
household. There Luther would dole out thoughts on anything to
eager students at the dinner-table (much of it recorded as his *Table
Talk*); there he wrote his hundreds of letters of pastoral advice.
Like his theology, his advice is consistently startling:

Whenever the devil pesters you with these thoughts, at once seek out
the company of men, drink more, joke and jest, or engage in some other
form of merriment. Sometimes it is necessary to drink a little more, play,
jest, or even commit some sin in defiance and contempt of the devil in
order not to give him an opportunity to make us scrupulous about trifles.
We shall be overcome if we worry too much about falling into some sin.

Accordingly if the devil should say, 'Do not drink,' you should reply
to him, 'On this very account, because you forbid it, I shall drink, and
what is more, I shall drink a generous amount.' Thus one must always
do the opposite of that which Satan prohibits. What do you think is
my reason for drinking wine undiluted, talking freely, and eating more
often if it is not to torment and vex the devil who made up his mind to

5. 'Second Sermon, 10 March 1522, Monday after Invocavit', *Luther's Works*,
vol. 51, p. 77.

torment and vex me? Would that I could commit some token sin simply for the sake of mocking the devil, so that he might understand that I acknowledge no sin and am conscious of no sin. When the devil attacks and torments us, we must completely set aside the whole Decalogue. When the devil throws our sins up to us and declares that we deserve death and hell, we ought to speak thus: 'I admit that I deserve death and hell. What of it? Does this mean that I shall be sentenced to eternal damnation? By no means. For I know One who suffered and made satisfaction in my behalf. His name is Jesus Christ, the Son of God. Where he is, there I shall be also.'[6]

Luther knew that, for all the political support he might receive, the Reformation would be a superficial thing if it did not win hearts and minds. The first need, then, was for a translation of the entire Bible that everyone could read in their own German. This he provided, richly illustrated, in 1534. For Luther, the Bible is our supreme authority. While even prophets and apostles could and have erred, the Bible as God's Word never does. It authenticates and interprets itself, never needing anything external for its validation, nor surrendering its authority to any other source of information. He was adamant that the Bible is clear and self-evidently intelligible. Without it, God cannot be truly known. For this reason, the vast majority of Luther's theology is biblical commentary (and most of that on the Old Testament).

Luther was no bibliolater, though. His attitude to the Bible was governed by his view that its sole content and message, from Genesis to Revelation, is Christ. So strongly did he maintain this that he made the test of a book's canonicity whether it teaches Christ, not who wrote it. It was because he felt that the apostle James's letter was not sufficiently clear in its proclamation of Christ that he wrote, 'I almost feel like throwing Jimmy into the stove'.[7]

---

6. To Jerome Weller, July 1530, in *Luther: Letters of Spiritual Counsel*, Library of Christian Classics, ed. T. G. Tappert (Vancouver: Regent College, 2003), pp. 86–87.

7. 'The Licentiate Examination of Heinrich Schmedenstede', *Luther's Works*, vol. 34, p. 317; cf. pp. 362, 396.

Even the Old Testament section of his translation was filled with woodcut illustrations of Christ, for he believed that Christ was actually present with the Old Testament believers, whom he called 'Christians'. Their faith was in no way pre-Christian; rather, they had faith in Christ and wrote their prophecies about him. It was this belief that undergirded Luther's most notorious writings against the Jews. In 1523 he had written a tract that condemned the persecution of Jews, advocating instead that Christians use the Old Testament to prove to them Jesus' messiahship. Yet by 1542 he had come to see a devilish stubbornness in the Jewish refusal to acknowledge that their own Scriptures spoke so clearly of Christ. He therefore wrote *On the Jews and Their Lies*, advocating the application of blasphemy laws to Jews. This would entail the destruction of synagogues and the expulsion of the Jews. Unsurprisingly, the Nazis sought to justify their anti-Semitism with this (Luther having become a national hero for his stand against the foreign power of Rome and his Bible translation's shaping of the German language). One could wish Luther had never written the work. It is, without doubt, the most unpleasant product of a pen that could pour forth obscene scatological vulgarity at his opponents. However, for all that, twentieth-century anti-Semitism is too often read back into Luther incorrectly. Nazism developed its racism out of nineteenth-century Darwinism and Romanticism, not Lutheranism.[8] Luther's intolerance of the Jews was not racial but spiritual, based on what he saw as their refusal to acknowledge the clear Christian meaning of the Old Testament. Thus, while he became entirely intolerant of Jews who rejected Christ, he could aid and befriend those who converted.

For Luther, the written word should not exist without becoming a spoken word, a word talked about and understood by the people.

---

8. 'Luther's antagonism to the Jews was poles apart from the Nazi doctrine of "Race" . . . I suppose Hitler never once read a page by Luther. The fact that he and other Nazis claimed Luther on their side proves no more than the fact that they also numbered Almighty God among their supporters' (Gordon Rupp, *Martin Luther: Hitler's Cause or Cure?* [London: Lutterworth, 1945], pp. 75, 84).

He thus corrected abuses in the liturgy and rewrote it to make it a Bible teacher. He also wrote two catechisms, the Large Catechism for adults and the Small Catechism for children, introducing the Ten Commandments (law) to illuminate sin; the Apostles' Creed (gospel) to apply forgiveness; the Lord's Prayer as our prayerful response; and the two sacraments as means of grace to sustain the believer. Then, applying his belief in the priesthood of all believers, he introduced congregational singing (where previously the congregation had been mere spectators). Everyone would now sing of God's truth. And it would be important for Luther that they were singing it: Luther believed music to be of next importance after theology. Like the word and the sacraments, he viewed music as an external thing that affects the heart; like them it chases away the devil, dispersing the spiritual anxieties he attacks us with. Luther even wrote a number of hymns, the most famous being that battlehymn of the Reformation, 'A Mighty Fortress is our God'.

Spearheading the Reformation under a death sentence, and with repeated attacks on his theology and life, it is no wonder that his health cracked. For ten years or so it declined until, in the cold winter of 1546, it gave out and Luther died, excommunicated from the church he had hoped to reform. His last written words were 'We are beggars. That is true.' They sum up so much of his thought: we are nothing but spiritual beggars who contribute nothing to our salvation or understanding of God; but there is, outside ourselves, God's word of truth. On that we depend.

Luther's thought

To feel the bite of Luther's theological revolution, we need to track the development of his thought in those crucial early years. Only then does it become clear that his was a truly theological revolution, and not merely a protest at abuses. Only then is the staggering and disturbing radicality of his proposal made clear.

Perhaps more than anything else, the years leading up to the 'tower experience' of 1519 see the development of his theology of the cross. In his lectures of 1515–16 on Romans, his theology of the cross was that God's blessing comes to us only through his condemnation

of us. Our problem is that, full of self-love, we naturally attempt to
use God in order to get and enjoy heaven for ourselves. The only
remedy for such self-love is self-accusation, for it is only when we
resign ourselves to hell in submission to God's condemnation of us
that we can say that we are loving God for his own sake, and not for
the gifts or the heaven he can give us. Freely handing ourselves over
to damnation, we are submitting to God, and are clearly no longer
just using God for his gifts. This, then, was a form of justification by
faith alone, but the faith is in his condemnation of us, not his gospel-
word of free salvation. What distinguishes it from Luther's mature
doctrine of justification is that it does not have the passive quality
he would later give it. Where later it would involve simple belief in
God's declaration of forgiveness, here it looked more like an exercise
in humility: we are justified by condemning ourselves. Thus he can
talk still of striving to be made righteous, and of becoming more and
more righteous – language he would later renounce.

In 1518 Luther was invited to explain his theology to the
German congregation of his Augustinian order in Heidelberg.
Although the Heidelberg Disputation caused less of a stir than his
ninety-five theses, it was in the end far more influential theologic-
ally. Six future Reformers were present to hear Luther. There he
expounded a substantially developed theology of the cross that
was to underlie all his mature thought (despite the fact that still he
had not understood justification as he later would). His theological
argument consisted of four steps:[9]

Theses 1–12: The problem of good works

Luther begins with a refusal to allow that any human works have
intrinsic merit before God. Instead he argues that, naturally, our
best works are nothing but damnable sins. To explain this he
brings in a sharp distinction between law and gospel that he would
always maintain. For Luther, law is not limited to Sinai or the Old
Testament; it is all that accuses us of sin. We cannot be saved by

---

9. For this structure I am indebted to the analysis of Gerhard O. Forde, *On
   Being a Theologian of the Cross: Reflections on Luther's Heidelberg Disputation, 1518*
   (Grand Rapids: Eerdmans, 1997).

doing the good works demanded by the law. Instead, 'law brings the wrath of God, kills, reviles, accuses, judges, and condemns everything that is not in Christ'.[10] To think that any work of ours might advance our righteousness before God is to confuse law with gospel. The gospel, in contrast, is a proclamation that the law's demands have been met in Christ, and, similarly, is not limited to the New Testament. Yet the gospel's message of salvation can be understood only by first hearing the law's pronouncement of the judgment we need saving from. Christians then find themselves living in a tension between law and gospel: as sinners we feel the law's accusation, yet through faith in Christ we fulfil the law.

Theses 13–18: The problem of the will
Having ruled out any merit in our works, Luther delves to the real problem: the corrupt human will, which can produce only corrupt human works. Ever since the Fall we have sought a freedom for our wills that is entirely unbounded, even by God. This is sin. So, with our works condemned and our very wills incapable of pleasing God, what can we do? Luther says, 'fall down and pray for grace'.[11] Thus he reveals that he had not yet attained his mature understanding. Here grace still comes by something we do (by prayer). In his mature understanding, grace comes through accepting God's promise; we remain entirely passive.

Theses 19–24: The way of glory versus the way of the cross
Luther then outlines the essential difference between his theology and the one he is opposing. The theology of glory is the theology of the natural man, who believes that works are good, suffering is bad and that we need no more than some encouragement to raise ourselves up to God. In shattering contrast, the theology of the cross attacks all those things that we believe to be the best in religion, showing that we cannot raise ourselves up, that the cross is our desert, and that only through suffering death can glory be reached. Thus we are reduced to utter dependence on Christ and his way of the cross.

---

10. 'Heidelberg Disputation, Thesis 23', *Luther's Works*, vol. 31, p. 54.
11. 'Heidelberg Disputation, Thesis 16', ibid. p. 50.

Theses 25–28: God creates us out of nothing
All that said, the theology of the cross presupposes resurrection. This is its goal: the sinner must be reduced to nothing – he must die – before he can receive new life. God only creates life out of nothing; he never looks to build on our foundations. 'The love of God does not find, but creates, that which is pleasing to it.'[12]

This theology of the cross was to provide the dynamics of all his thinking to come.[13] The point is that God clothes himself to come to us (whether in the incarnation, the Bible or the sacraments), yet his appearance is the complete opposite of what we would expect. We expect him to be pleased with us and our works; we expect him to be like us. Yet the truth is hidden in an alien disguise, and thus, to the blinded sinner, God appears to be the devil, and the devil appears to be the lord of the world. Even what we receive from God (the cross, death, suffering, the world's hatred etc.) is the opposite of what we would expect from him. This being the case, Luther would always exploit the paradoxes and contrasts of the gospel as far as he could.

The life of faith is thus one of constant *Anfechtung* (conflict or temptation) as we believe in opposition to our hearts, minds and consciences. 'To believe means to live in constant contradiction of empirical reality and to trust one's self to that which is hidden.'[14] Our hearts believe that our works can please God. Faith says otherwise. Our consciences condemn us, since we are sinners. Faith turns to the gospel, for only there can we know the truth about ourselves. Faith trusts Christ instead of the heart or the conscience.

Finally, for Luther, faith contradicts reason, and this requires some more detailed examination. Luther was not attacking the proper use of the mind, but the presumption of the mind to think

---

12. 'Heidelberg Disputation, Thesis 28', ibid. p. 57.
13. As he put it, *CRUX sola est nostra theologia* (the cross alone is our theology); indeed, *crux probat omnia* (the cross tests all) (*Luther's Commentary on the First Twenty-Two Psalms*, tr. J. N. Lenker [Sunbury, Pa.: Lutherans in All Lands, 1903], vol. 1, pp. 289, 294–295).
14. P. Althaus, *The Theology of Martin Luther*, tr. R. C. Schultz (Philadelphia: Fortress, 1966), p. 33.

that it could know God and his ways unaided by revelation. He
described scholastic and natural theology as enemies of the cross
in just the same sense as moralism.[15] They are all, he believed,
forms of Pelagianism. Without revelation, the human mind does
not even know what its own sin is, because it does not know the
God that sin offends. The only God it can imagine is the devil.
The true God is a God who is revealed. He is revealed only in

---

15. J. I. Packer pulls together a number of Luther's concerns as he explains,
'It was in her capacity as the prompter and agent of "natural" theology
that Mistress Reason was in Luther's eyes the Devil's whore; for natural
theology is, he held, blasphemous in principle, and bankrupt in practice.
It is blasphemous in principle, because it seeks to snatch from God a
knowledge of Himself which is not His gift, but man's achievement – a
triumph of human brain-power; thus it would feed man's pride, and exalt
him above his Creator, as one who could know God at pleasure, whether
or not God willed to be known by him. Thus natural theology appears
as one more attempt on man's part to implement the programme which
he espoused in his original sin – to deny his creaturehood, and deify
himself, and deal with God henceforth on an independent footing. But
natural theology is bankrupt in practice; for it never brings its devotees to
God; instead it leaves them stranded in a quaking morass of insubstantial
speculation. Natural theology leads men away from the Divine Christ, and
from Scripture, the cradle in which He lies, and from the *theologia crucis*,
the gospel doctrine which sets Christ forth. But it is only through Christ
that God wills to be known, and gives saving knowledge of Himself. He
who would know God, therefore, must seek Him through the Biblical
gospel . . . Man is by nature as completely unable to know God as to
please God; let him face the fact and admit it! Let God be God! let man
be man! let ruined sinners cease pretending to be something other than
ruined sinners! let them realise that they lie helpless in the hand of an
angry Creator; let them seek Christ, and cry for mercy. This is the point
of Luther's polemic against reason. It takes its place as a part of his all-
embracing prophetic onslaught against the proud vainglory of helpless
sinners who deny their own helplessness' (J. I. Packer and O. R. Johnston,
'Historical and Theological Introduction' to *Martin Luther on The Bondage of
the Will* [Cambridge: James Clarke, 1957], pp. 46–47).

Christ, the God on the cross, made known in the Old and New Testaments, which preach him. Even then, we sinners can only know him when we are reduced to nothing and die with him on the cross. Thus, he can write, there is 'only one article and one rule of theology, and this is true faith or trust in Christ'.[16]

In some ways Luther's serious spiritual anxiety really began with the sacraments, when he conducted that first mass; in 1519 it was the sacraments that helped him solve his crisis. In a sermon on penance (which he still viewed as the third sacrament), he argued against the official view that said it was a presumption to assume one had definitely received grace through the sacrament. Luther retorted that God promised grace through the sacraments, and that therefore it was a sin to deny what God had promised. Ironically, Luther was, in a sense, defending a higher view of the sacraments than Rome! Yet this formed the structure of his gospel-discovery. He saw in the sacraments something external, outside himself, that promised God's grace. This, he saw, was the nature of the gospel: we do not look to ourselves; we look to something external, the promise of God, and by receiving that, receive his grace. When next he turned to Romans 1:17, he could understand the righteousness of God to be something passively received in a way he never had before.

The year after that final piece fell into place, 1520, was a year of extraordinary productivity for Luther. He produced a number of popularly accessible tracts to promote and explain the theology of the new Reformation: *Treatise on Good Works*, *To the Christian Nobility of the German Nation*, *The Babylonian Captivity of the Church* and *The Freedom of a Christian*.

Treatise on Good Works
Luther needed to establish that his theology was not about devaluing good works, and so in this first treatise set out his own analysis of the Ten Commandments. Underpinning it all is Luther's distinction between the mere outward appearance of obedience to

---

16. *Table Talk*, no. 1583: 'The Tempted and Afflicted Understand the Gospel', Between 20 and 27 May 1532, *Luther's Works*, vol. 54, p. 157.

the commandments, through works, and real obedience through faith. What matters is our trust in Christ. Only born out of that trust can any of our works be good, for only then do we honour God's name and not ours. This is because faith acknowledges who God is and what he is like. In other words, faith is true worship. And that being the case, holiness can be cultivated only through the preaching of the gospel:

> In fact, when we see it properly, love comes first, or at any rate it comes at the same time as faith. For I could not have faith in God if I did not think he wanted to be favorable and kind to me. This in turn makes me feel kindly disposed toward him, and I am moved to trust him with all my heart and to look to him for all good things . . . Look here! This is how you must cultivate Christ in yourself, and see how in him God holds before you his mercy and offers it to you without any prior merits of your own. It is from such a view of his grace that you must draw faith and confidence in the forgiveness of all your sins. Faith, therefore, does not originate in works; neither do works create faith, but faith must spring up and flow from the blood and wounds and death of Christ. If you see in these that God is so kindly disposed toward you that he even gives his own Son for you, then your heart in turn must grow sweet and disposed toward God . . . We never read that the Holy Spirit was given to anybody because he had performed some works, but always when men have heard the gospel of Christ and the mercy of God.[17]

All that being the case, there can no longer be any hierarchy of works. Whether staying at home, fasting or going to church, what matters is the state of the heart towards God. Has the work been done out of a heartfelt love for God, sprung from a knowledge of his love for me?

To the Christian Nobility of the German Nation

Luther believed that, in order to safeguard her power, Rome had built three defensive theological walls around herself: she asserted first that all earthly rulers had to bow to the pope as the supreme

---

17. 'Treatise on Good Works', *Luther's Works*, vol. 44, pp. 30, 38–39.

temporal power; secondly, that only the pope might interpret the Scriptures; thirdly, that no one but the pope could summon a council and thus reform the church. These Luther now sought to bring down with a blast of his pen.

His essential move was to destroy the distinction between clergy and laity. This stripped away any rationale for the pope's being the supreme temporal power. It also allowed every Christian the right to interpret Scripture and to call a council to reform the church. For this last point Luther enjoyed playing a trump card: Nicea, the most important council in church history, had been called by a layman, the emperor Constantine.

This being the case, Luther could call on the ruling classes of Germany to protect the spiritual, as well as temporal, welfare of their people against the ravages of Rome. In practice, Luther got what he sought: the Reformation in Germany could never have thrived as it did without the protection of the princes, many of whom became its patrons. Nine years after the Diet of Worms, a number of the German princes who had watched Luther's defence before Charles V presented the Augsburg Confession of Lutheran faith to the same emperor for his approval. There were consequences, however, that Luther did not intend. Having effectively set up the German princes as emergency bishops, unwittingly he had steered subsequent Lutheranism onto a course in which churches would exist subservient to governments.

What Luther proposed was a theology of government derived from Augustine's idea of the two cities (of God and man). In keeping with the other dualities in his thought (gospel and law, inner faith and outer works, the way of glory and the way of the cross etc.), Luther developed a distinction between the kingdom of God and the kingdom of the world. The kingdom of God is the church, God's instrument of mercy. In that kingdom, God rules hearts persuasively by his word. If everyone were to obey that word, there would be no need for the other kingdom. As it is, God provides the state as the kingdom of the world, his instrument of wrath against the disobedient. In that kingdom, God rules outward behaviour coercively by the sword. Through the kingdom of the world God restrains evil and exercises his providential care for all.

Rome, he argued, had confused the two kingdoms by making

the pope the lord of both. Yet Luther would never stand with the
radicals, who separated themselves from everything to do with the
state. Christians, he held, are citizens of both kingdoms, and are
to be active in both. The two kingdoms are to support each other:
as the prince protects the church, so the pastor urges the people
to obey the prince (so long as he is no tyrannical opponent of the
church). Then, he maintained, the gospel can flourish.

The Babylonian Captivity of the Church
Luther's new understanding of the gospel required a complete
break from Rome's sacramental system. The freedom of the
Christian could never be preserved when the church herself was
in captivity to it. Rome's spiritual power depended on the idea
that grace was administered automatically through the clergy's
performance of the sacraments. Luther's insistence on the need
for personal faith had already robbed the clergy of that control. In
The Babylonian Captivity of the Church he set about dismantling their
control further, by proposing a new theology of the sacraments.

Luther defined a sacrament as a word of promise from Christ,
accompanied by a sign. Sacraments, then, are words from God,
to be received by faith. He never ceased to value the sacraments
as powerful demonstrations of the external objectivity of God's
Word, as well as the fact that, as the sacraments are given to me,
personally, so God's promise is given to me, personally. (He would
go further, to say that as the sacraments are given to our bodies, so
the grace promised in them is meant also for our bodies.)

With this definition of a sacrament in place, Luther reduced
their number from seven to two. Marriage, he argued, is a gift to
all humanity, not a promise for believers only. Confirmation, while
acceptable, entails no promise from God, and therefore cannot be
classified as a sacrament. Extreme unction was instituted by the
apostle James, not Christ himself. The sacrament of ordination he
rejected for having no basis in Scripture (he accepted that some
believers should be authorized by God's people to teach God's
Word, but denied that that set them apart as an intermediary priesthood). Instead, he argued, all believers are priests, charged with
the duty to teach and spread God's Word. This left three sacraments: penance, baptism and the Lord's Supper. Giving a sense of

how fast his theology was moving, at the beginning of the work Luther treats penance as a valid third sacrament, but by the end excludes it on the grounds that it has no external sign. This left baptism and the Lord's Supper.

Baptism, he maintained, is a promise of new life in Christ, signified by water. Having received the promise, we are called to respond to it in faith. This distinguished his position from Rome's, but it would also lead him into conflict with the new radicals and 'Anabaptists' (literally 'rebaptizers'). Many of the radicals rejected all sacraments because of their externality (thus, Luther wrote, rejecting how God himself has willed to deal with us). The Anabaptists rejected infant baptism (and thus would seek to baptize adults who had already been baptized as infants). Luther's response to the Anabaptists was a clear example of his overall theology in action. He believed that their rejection of infant baptism compromised the gospel, for it made one's own confession of faith, rather than God's Word, the essential thing. For Luther, it looked like a return to dependence on something internal, so letting faith become a work. It was pastorally vital for him that God's promise in baptism was in no way dependent on anything within a person: when troubled in conscience it was Luther's habit to write on his desk in chalk *baptizatus sum* (I am baptized). His consolation was always external; he would never trust even his own faith, but only direct that faith at God's objective Word.

Luther believed that the other sacrament, of bread and wine, had been taken captive by Rome in a number of ways: Rome forbade the laity from receiving the wine out of fear that it might be spilt; she taught that the mass is a new sacrifice or good work before God; and she taught the doctrine of transubstantiation. Justification by faith alone and the resultant priesthood of all believers dealt with the first two errors. His objection to transubstantiation was that it was an Aristotelian, as opposed to biblical, doctrine whereby the earthly (bread and wine) is entirely replaced by the heavenly (body and blood). It also propagated an individualism among those who individually received its benefits, whereas the true sacrament of the Lord's Supper creates communion.

The disagreement with Rome over the Lord's Supper was not to be Luther's last word on the subject. In fact, after justification, the Lord's Supper was the doctrine Luther gave most time to. This was largely because of his disagreement with other Reformers, especially Zwingli of Zurich. Zwingli argued that Christ's body is not literally present in the sacrament, but is instead symbolized by the bread. The Lord's Supper, he believed, was a mere symbol to help us commemorate Christ's sacrifice and signify our membership of his body. This was entirely unacceptable to Luther, who believed that Zwingli had hardened his heart against the clear words of Christ: 'This is my body.' The result, thought Luther, was that Zwingli fell into the same error as the Anabaptists, of replacing grace with works and converting the sacrament into an opportunity for us to do something (i.e. remember Christ and signify something about us). Such a view simply could not be reconciled with Luther's understanding. Luther maintained that Christ's body and blood are really present and given to all in the bread and wine, to the harm of those who refuse to trust him, but to the blessing of those who receive him by faith.

The Freedom of a Christian

Perhaps even more remarkable than his output in 1520 was the fact that, only two weeks after the appearance of his incendiary *Against the Execrable Bull of Antichrist* he produced one of the most beautiful and positive statements of evangelical theology – and addressed it to the pope! 'I have never thought ill of you personally,' he wrote, for 'I have no quarrels with any man concerning his morals but only concerning the word of truth.' This, despite the fact that he could still tell the pope that

> the Roman church, once the holiest of all, has become the most
> licentious den of thieves [Matt. 21:13], the most shameless of all
> brothels, the kingdom of sin, death, and hell. It is so bad that even
> Antichrist himself, if he should come, could think of nothing to add
> to its wickedness.[18]

Luther was seeking to rescue the pope himself from Rome!

---

18. 'The Freedom of a Christian', ibid. vol. 31, pp. 335–336.

The Freedom of a Christian is organized around two propos-itions: 'A Christian is a perfectly free lord of all, subject to none. A Christian is a perfectly dutiful servant of all, subject to all.'[19]

Inward freedom

The work depends heavily on the story of the lover and his beloved in Song of Songs (especially 2:16, 'My lover is mine and I am his'), understood as an allegory of Christ and his church. Luther likens the gospel to the story of a prostitute who marries a king.

First, the marriage is effected by the wedding vow. Just so, Christ gives himself to us through his own promise. This was at the heart of Luther's departure from Augustine (or at least the earlier and more Catholic side of Augustine). Augustine had held that God gives grace to those who pray for it. Luther held that grace is given, not on the basis of what we say, but what God says. We receive grace by believing God's promise. When we accept the word, we receive all that belongs to the word. It might be more helpful to describe this as 'justification by God's word' instead of 'justification by faith', because it is God's word that justifies here, not our faith as such. Pastorally this was revolutionary, for in contrast to the introspective piety he had grown up with, Luther would always point doubters outwards to God's sure word, not inwards to their own fickle faith.

Secondly, upon the declaration of the wedding vow, the prosti-tute finds that she has been made a queen. It is not that she has in any way made her behaviour or character more queenly; it is that now she has been given a new status. Just so with the believer: because of an external word she receives a righteous status that is also external to her, and unrelated to her character and behaviour. Or, as Luther put it, her righteousness is both alien (external) and passive (unearned). And so, as the prostitute remains wayward in heart but a queen by status, so the believer is simultaneously right-eous and a sinner (*simul justus et peccator*), and will always remain so (*semper justus et peccator*).

The prostitute did not marry the king for his crown or wealth, and yet when she accepts him she also receives them. So the believer,

---

19. Ibid. p. 344.

when she accepts Christ, receives all that is his, just as he takes all that is hers (her sin). Then she can confidently display 'her sins in the face of death and hell and say, "If I have sinned, yet my Christ, in whom I believe, has not sinned, and all his is mine and all mine is his."'[20] Yet the believer has received Christ himself, and not merely his status. He, then, sets about the transformation of the heart of the believer such that she becomes increasingly righteous herself. Thus by faith she receives the Christ who both justifies and sanctifies.[21]

Luther's argument entailed a different understanding of faith from that of the Roman Catholicism of the day. In Catholicism, faith was essentially an assent that meant attending mass. For Luther it became personal trust in Christ; and, because he had demonstrated the idolatry of any good works done without faith, he had come to see faith as the only worship that pleases God.

This gave Luther an infinitely more powerful definition of sin. Sin, he saw, is essentially unbelief. 'The worst sin is not to accept the Word.'[22] This is the ultimate sin against the first commandment, for it refuses to take God seriously for who he is:

what greater contempt of God is there than not believing his promise? For what is this but to make God a liar or to doubt that he is truthful? – that is, to ascribe truthfulness to one's self but lying and vanity to God? Does not a man who does this deny God and set himself up as an idol in his heart?'[23]

---

20. Ibid. p. 352.
21. It is necessary to note that Christ himself is received into the believer's heart as well as the believer's being clothed externally with Christ's righteousness. A historical overemphasis on the latter has led to a fascinating and hotly debated reappraisal of the subject by some Finnish Luther scholars who reject the idea that Luther had a forensic understanding of justification (see C. E. Braaten and R. W. Jenson [eds.], *Union with Christ: The New Finnish Interpretation of Luther* [Grand Rapids: Eerdmans, 1998]).
22. 'Lectures on Isaiah, Chapters 40–66', *Luther's Works*, vol. 17, p. 383.
23. 'The Freedom of a Christian', ibid. vol. 31, p. 350.

No good works could avail one who had committed this sin of sins. Such works could only compound the idolatry by the implicit suggestion that they could create righteousness and life. Given this, it is small wonder that the believer should experience *Anfechtung* when she looks away from Christ to her own self and achievements, thus for a while failing to trust Christ. To look to one's self and one's work is not to have faith.

Luther believed that the failure to grasp this lay behind all the rotten structure of Rome. Like the Pharisee who had built his own idolatrous self-confidence on the failures of the tax collector, Rome's moralism only served to foster competition between individuals and thus hierarchy. Yet when faith becomes the only worship, all are levelled. Only then is there genuine community.

Outward subjection

If the first proposition ('A Christian is a perfectly free lord of all, subject to none') was concerned with faith, the second proposition ('A Christian is a perfectly dutiful servant of all, subject to all') looks at the true role of good works. For all the strength of his polemic against the misuse of works, Luther is no advocate for licence. Put simply, Luther sees good works as the natural result of justification, but never its cause. The prostitute/queen, though only queen because of her husband, now becomes queenly and begins to represent her husband to all; just so, since we now know and love Christ, we become Christs to our neighbours, serving them as Christ serves us, and thus representing him. The Christian, therefore, 'lives in Christ through faith, in his neighbor through love. By faith he is caught up beyond himself into God. By love he descends beneath himself into his neighbor.'[24]

The Bondage of the Will

In the very earliest days of Luther's protest against Rome, there seemed to be an alliance between the Reformer and a number of

---

24. Ibid. p. 371.

Renaissance scholars, such as Erasmus. Luther had used Erasmus' printing of the New Testament for his translation into German, and Erasmus initially welcomed Luther as a much-needed new broom who could clean up the corruption of Rome. The alliance, however, was entirely superficial, for while Erasmus attacked Rome's moral and practical abuses, Luther was attacking Rome's doctrine. Erasmus had little interest in theology, but he was soon disturbed by what he saw flowing from Luther's prolific pen.

Eventually, in 1524, he wrote *The Freedom of the Will*, arguing in effect that Luther had gone too far, that the sinner is merely weak-willed, and does have some ability to perform actions that are genuinely pleasing to God. If man had no freedom of choice, how could he ever have any merit before God? Why would God ever command anything of us? Erasmus had not exactly intended it, but what Luther saw was that *The Freedom of the Will* was a direct attack on *The Freedom of the Christian* – on the heart of the Reformation, in fact:

> you alone have attacked the real issue, the essence of the matter in dispute, and have not wearied me with irrelevancies about the papacy, purgatory, indulgences, and such like trifles (for trifles they are rather than basic issues), with which almost everyone hitherto has gone hunting for me without success. You and you alone have seen the question on which everything hinges, and have aimed at the vital spot; for which I sincerely thank you.[25]

To protect *The Freedom of a Christian*, Luther thus wrote *The Bondage of the Will*.

Luther saw that, if the sinner has in fact some basic ability to produce for himself a righteousness before God, then our salvation cannot be from God's grace alone, meaning that salvation is not received by faith alone. Erasmus, of course, had brought in our own contribution to our salvation with extreme subtlety; but in Luther's eyes that only

---

25. 'The Bondage of the Will', *Luther's Works*, vol. 33, p. 294.

made it more dangerous. It was a concealed trapdoor of Pelagianism.[26]

Luther thus set out to prove the absolute impossibility of the idea that naturally we might ever even desire to love and please God. He was not suggesting that we are unable to adhere to social norms and codes of morality, only that that is something quite different from having any true desire to love God. This inability of ours, he argued, comes from the fact that our wills are simply not free in that way. Here people are commonly confused. Luther never meant that somehow we are pushed into sin: 'when a man is without the Spirit of God he does not do evil against his will, as if he were taken by the scruff of the neck and forced to it'.[27] Quite the opposite: we freely choose to do the things we do. We do what we want. The trouble is, we never naturally want God, and our choices are entirely tied to that. We freely choose to do the things we love, but we are unable to choose *what* to love, and since we do not love God, we cannot choose for him. The only solution is for God in his grace to change our hearts and their desires; only then, finding that we love him, will we choose him.

All this simply expressed what Luther had found for himself. When, as a monk, he had thought of God as one who merely judges and demands perfection. Luther said, 'I did not love, yes, I hated the righteous God who punishes sinners, and secretly, if not blasphemously, certainly murmuring greatly, I was angry with God.'[28] All his zeal to serve God and win heaven only drove him to hate God more. But, through the gospel of God's loving and free grace, his heart was changed, and only then did he find he could love God and choose him. As he put it soon after, 'When this faith is rightly present the heart must be made glad by the testament. The heart must grow warm and melt in the love

---

26. Pelagianism, which is essentially the belief that we can (and must) save ourselves by our own efforts, is discussed in *The Breeze of the Centuries* (Nottingham: IVP, 2010), pp. 96–100.

27. 'The Bondage of the Will', *Luther's Works*, vol. 33, p. 64.

28. 'Preface to the Complete Edition of Luther's Latin Writings', ibid. vol. 34, pp. 336–337.

of God. Then praise and thanksgiving will follow with a pure heart.'[29]

Going on with Luther

Luther is effortless to read: he is stimulating, amusing and clear. Thus it could not be easier to deal with the man himself. Timothy Lull's anthology *Martin Luther's Basic Theological Writings* (Minneapolis: Fortress, 1989) contains an excellent collection of the most important works. *The Freedom of a Christian* is probably the place to start (also available on www.great-theologians.org). One slight shame is that space did not allow Lull to include the full text of *The Bondage of the Will*; this can be found, along with an outstanding introductory essay by J. I. Packer, in *Martin Luther on The Bondage of the Will*, ed. J. I. Packer and O. R. Johnston (Cambridge: James Clarke, 1957). Luther's *Letters of Spiritual Counsel* (Vancouver: Regent College, 2003) and *Table Talk*, both easily available, add some of the best vignettes of insight into the humanity of the man himself.

There are two books of essential readings in the secondary literature. The first is Roland Bainton's classic biography of Luther, *Here I Stand: A Life of Martin Luther* (Nashville: Abingdon, 1950). Though published in 1950, it is still an addictive read, and also attractively illustrated with contemporary woodcut illustrations. The other is Paul Althaus's *The Theology of Martin Luther*, tr. R. C. Schultz (Philadelphia: Fortress, 1966). It remains the best single-volume overview of Luther's theology, but is worth reading just for the material on sin and justification, irrespective of relevance to Luther himself!

---

29. 'Treatise on Good Works', ibid. vol. 44, p. 56.

Martin Luther timeline

1483 Luther born in Eisleben
1505 Thunderstorm; joins Augustinian monastery in Erfurt
1511 Moves to Wittenberg
1517 Posts the ninety-five theses on the door of the Castle Church in Wittenberg
1518 Heidelberg disputation
1519 'Tower experience'
1520 Writes *Treatise on Good Works, To the Christian Nobility of the German Nation, The Babylonian Captivity of the Church, Against the Execrable Bull of Antichrist, The Freedom of the Christian*; burns the papal bull excommunicating him
1521 Diet of Worms; taken into protective custody in the Wartburg Castle, Eisenach, where he translates the New Testament into German
1522 Returns to Wittenberg
1524 Peasants' War begins; Erasmus writes *On the Freedom of the Will*
1525 Writes *On the Bondage of the Will*; marries Katharina von Bora
1529 Luther and Zwingli fail to agree on the Lord's Supper at the Marburg Colloquy
1530 Lutheran princes present the *Augsburg Confession* of Lutheran belief to the emperor at the Diet of Augsburg
1534 First complete edition of Luther's translation of the Bible
1546 Luther dies visiting his home town of Eisleben

2. KNOWING A LOVING GOD

John Calvin

Geneva: today it is an international symbol of peace and stability, but even to mention the city in the sixteenth century was to invite argument. For some it was a shining beacon of gospel hope; for others it was a hotbed of revolution, a nest of heresy. All this because of one man: John Calvin. Today we tend to know more about Calvinism than Calvin himself. Yet still the man manages to polarize opinion. On the one hand there are those who see him in stained glass; on the other are those for whom he was Geneva's cantankerous and cruel dictator, a man whose belief in a terrifying God inspired a reign of religious terror. 'Better with Beza in hell than with Calvin in heaven!' as his enemies used to say. Of course, neither picture is accurate. In fact, the real problem with Calvin is how enigmatic he was. He was extraordinarily reticent about speaking of himself, and, lacking Luther's white-hot charisma, his personality has become much harder to make out down through the centuries.

What we can know more easily is his theology. And when the caricatures are left to one side, Calvin can be appreciated as a theologian who has much to offer both those who call themselves Calvinist and those who do not. Karl Barth put it like this:

Calvin is a cataract, a primeval forest, a demonic power, something directly down from Himalaya, absolutely Chinese, strange, mythological; I lack completely the means, the suction cups, even to assimilate this phenomenon, not to speak of presenting it adequately. What I receive is only a thin little stream and what I can then give out again is only a yet thinner extract of this little stream. I could gladly and profitably set myself down and spend all the rest of my life just with Calvin.[1]

Calvin's life

Jean Cauvin, as he was known before he Latinized his name, was born on 10 July 1509 in Noyon, some 60 miles north of Paris. Intended by his father for the priesthood, at the age of eleven or twelve he was sent to the University of Paris to study theology. About five years later his father changed his mind and withdrew Jean from Paris, sending him instead to Orléans to study law. There he was introduced to a new world of humanism, and made friends with a group sympathetic to the ideas of renaissance and church reform.[2] Some of these, such as Melchior Wolmar and Calvin's cousin Pierre Robert, were actually committed to the Reformation.

At this time Wolmar taught Calvin Greek, which was highly significant. Greek was a language intimately associated with the Reformation, Greek being used to challenge the church's Latin Vulgate translation and thus challenge the authority of the church itself. As T. H. L. Parker puts it, 'Greek spelt the beginning of the

1. Karl Barth to Eduard Thurneysen, 8 June 1922. Barth uses the term 'demonic' in its original sense here, meaning that Calvin was a supernatural force. No connotation of evil is implied!
2. Sixteenth-century humanism has nothing to do with twentieth-century secular humanism. Humanism then was a movement dedicated to the rediscovery of classical Greek and Latin culture. Its motto, *Ad fontes!* (To the Sources!) showed its aim: humanism sought to drink directly from the clear intellectual waters of antiquity rather than from what it saw as the stagnant pond of constipated medieval scholasticism.

end for the Latin church, at least in its then form.'[3] At any rate, it was around this time that, as Calvin later wrote, 'God by a sudden conversion subdued and brought my mind to a teachable frame.'[4] Surprisingly, we know no more than that about the conversion of the great Reformer. We can only say that it is highly likely that it was brought about through his reading of Luther's 1520 Reformation treatises.

There was one other telling event during those years: Calvin wrote a commentary on the Roman philosopher Seneca's call for the emperor Nero to exercise clemency (*De clementia*). More than anything it was an attempt by Calvin to make his mark as a humanist scholar. Yet it was to provide the foundation for all the biblical commentaries to come. Calvin would use all the critical and linguistic tools of humanism to develop a method of exegesis that is recognizably modern.

The time for enjoying such humanist study was soon to be over for Calvin, though. While he was back for a short time in Paris, the new rector of the university, Nicholas Cop, delivered an address that was considered heretically Lutheran. Before Cop could be arrested, he fled to Basel in Switzerland (a free city in favour of the Reformation, where Erasmus, Heinrich Bullinger, Guillaume Farel and Pierre Robert were already living). The authorities quickly came looking for Calvin, who was perhaps suspected of being Cop's ghostwriter. Apparently, Calvin only just escaped, lowered from the window on a rope of bed sheets.

It was not an easy time to be on the run in France; and with friends and co-Reformers being burned, the situation was getting more difficult by the day. Thus he made his way to join Cop in Basel. While there he helped Pierre Robert with his new French translation of the Bible and, incredibly, having been a Christian for no more than five years, completed the first edition of his *Institutes of the Christian Religion*.

If anything could be more momentous, it was to follow. After

---

3. T. H. L. Parker, *John Calvin: A Biography* (Oxford: Lion, 2006), p. 9.

4. Calvin's preface to his commentary on the Psalms (Edinburgh: Calvin Translation Society, 1844–56; repr. Grand Rapids: Baker, 1993), 1.40.

about a year he began travelling again with friends. Having made his way back to Paris, he intended to go on to Strasbourg, one of the major centres of the Reformation in Europe. However, the armies of Francis I and Charles V lay in the way, forcing him to take a long detour to the south. Calvin intended therefore to stop overnight in Geneva, a city which had recently become evangelical by constitution, but which was far from being settled in its evangelicalism. Unfortunately for Calvin, he was waylaid by the fiery Guillaume Farel, who begged him to help build up the church in Geneva. When Calvin replied that he wanted instead to devote himself to private study, Farel

> proceeded to utter an imprecation that God would curse my retirement, and the tranquillity of the studies which I sought, if I should withdraw and refuse to give assistance, when the necessity was so urgent. By this imprecation I was so stricken with terror, that I desisted from the journey which I had undertaken.[5]

So Calvin settled in Geneva (!), at first as an academic, but soon as a full-time pastor. Thus, like his hero Augustine, Calvin found himself dragged from the comfort of the study to the rigours of the pulpit.

However uncomfortable the shift might have felt, Calvin showed no signs of heel-dragging. With unnerving speed he and Farel set about the reformation of the church in Geneva. Unsurprisingly, this raised hackles, and the popular mood began to turn against them. They were accused of being French spies, and finally, when in 1538 they refused to obey the city council's order to use unleavened bread in the Easter Communion, they were banned from preaching and then expelled from Geneva.

Calvin believed that he had effectively ruined the church in Geneva and so had been removed from pastoral ministry by God. Yet this, of course, meant that he could resume the quiet life of scholarship from which Farel had dragged him two years earlier. And the perfect place for such a life was Strasbourg, his original destination. Geneva had been a mere interlude.

---

5. Ibid. 1.43.

One can only feel sorry for Calvin, for there in Strasbourg he was accosted by Martin Bucer, who followed Farel's example and called Calvin a Jonah for fleeing from his calling, urging him instead to the work of pastoring the many French refugees in the city. This Calvin did, and in the process learned more about the pastorate than he had from anyone else. The lessons learned in Strasbourg would profoundly shape Calvin's understanding of what a church should look like. Also during his time in Strasbourg, Calvin was invited to some of the great Protestant–Catholic dialogues, such as at Regensburg in 1541. There he was disappointed, not only by the concessions some Lutherans were prepared to make to Rome, but also by their lack of discipline and overdependence on the state. In the years to come they would serve as a warning in his mind as he sought to shape the church in Geneva.

Calvin's theological work hardly suffered from his pastoral demands. When the eminent Cardinal Sadoleto wrote a letter to Geneva inviting her to return to the Roman fold, the city council, despite having exiled Calvin, saddled him with the task of responding. In reply Calvin produced a tour de force of Reformation theology, vindicating it biblically and historically and exposing the weakness of Sadoleto's thought. He also produced his first major commentary (on Romans) and produced a substantially revised edition of his *Institutes*.

In Strasbourg his friends also sought to get him married. Calvin was hardly a natural romantic. He once wrote, 'I know not if I shall ever marry. If I did so, it would be in order to devote my time to the Lord, by being the more relieved from the worries of daily life.'[6] Yet in 1540 he came to marry Idelette de Bure, a sickly widow who brought with her two children from her former Anabaptist husband, and Calvin evidently loved her dearly. In 1542 they had a son, Jacques, who died after two weeks. The consolation Calvin received at this time from his strong doctrine of divine sovereignty is movingly evident from what he wrote to a

6. F. Wendel, *Calvin: The Origins and Development of his Religious Thought* (London: Collins, 1963), p. 65.

friend soon afterwards: 'The Lord has certainly inflicted a severe and bitter wound in the death of our baby son. But He is Himself a Father and knows best what is good for his children.'[7] In 1549 Idelette herself died, leaving Calvin to care for her two children.

Calvin was only to remain in Strasbourg for three years, for in that time the politics changed in Geneva, and then they wanted him back. He was extremely reluctant to return, but was again persuaded. And so, in 1541, Calvin returned to Geneva for good. As soon as he was back in the pulpit he simply resumed his sermon series at the verse where he had left off three years earlier. (Here was a preacher dedicated to sequential exposition!) Yet even before that, on the very day of his return, he submitted to the city council his Ecclesiastical Ordinances for the comprehensive reformation of the church in Geneva.

In them he proposed details such as that every family in Geneva had to receive a pastoral visit once a year and be catechized, only those who passed being admissible to communion. Perhaps the most important proposal, though, was for the establishment of a consistory, an ecclesiastical disciplinary committee. If Geneva was not to end up like the ill-disciplined Lutheran churches, if she was not to be associated with the city of Münster, he believed Geneva must be disciplined.[8] The proposals were largely accepted, and so a consistory was established. Essentially, its business consisted of giving practical instruction to individuals. For example, one recalcitrant family was directed 'to frequent the sermons and the catechism and to buy a Bible in their house and have it read'.[9]

---

7. Letter 90, to Viret, *The Letters of John Calvin*, tr. Jules Bonnet (New York: Franklin, 1972), vol. 4, p. 332.

8. In 1534 radical Anabaptists had seized control of the German city of Münster, turning it into a cultish and polygamous commune that had horrified all Europe. After a bloody siege the city was retaken, but for more than a century Münster cast a long shadow of suspicion over the idea of reforming cities.

9. *Registers of the Consistory of Geneva in the Time of Calvin*, vol. 1, 1542–4, ed. Robert M. Kingdon, Thomas A. Lambert and Isabella M. Watt, tr. M. Wallace McDonald (Grand Rapids: Eerdmans, 1996), p. 134.

Much of Calvin's bad reputation stems from the fact that the consistory could be overzealous: we read of disciplinary action taken against individuals for merely stating that the pope was a good man, for making a noise during a sermon, or for singing a rude song about Calvin, and so on. Certainly, it created a city very unlike Luther's Wittenberg: for a while inns in Geneva were forbidden for citizens, and in their place five 'abbeys' were provided in which guests were given a French Bible and placed under supervision.

Such moral policing exasperated many in Geneva, who often then reacted against Calvin personally. But did Calvin deserve his reputation as the moralizing despot? The fact is that he was never capable of being such a figure. Calvin was a mere resident alien in Geneva, not a citizen, and thus had no right to vote or hold any secular office. He could be dismissed or expelled at the whim of the city council. Despotic power was simply beyond his grasp, and his scholarly temperament makes the thought that he would ever have wanted it incredible.

The crucible for Calvin's reputation has always been the burning of Michael Servetus for heresy in 1553. Servetus' denial of the Trinity and consequent reconstruction of the doctrine of salvation was acknowledged by Catholic and Protestant alike to be spiritually homicidal heresy. Thus, after he escaped arrest for his views in Catholic France, it was hardly surprising when he was arrested upon arrival in Geneva. All Europe was watching, for the question was, would Geneva be more tolerant than Rome and countenance arch-heresy? Geneva itself was accused of being heretical; if she tolerated Servetus, it would prove the point. Thus the city council put Servetus on trial, calling on Calvin to act as their prosecutor. However, we should not imagine Calvin to be the puppet-master behind it all; at the time the council were so hostile to Calvin that Servetus thought he could get Calvin banished instead of himself. The council consulted with other Protestant cities in Switzerland and Germany: all agreed that Servetus should be sentenced to death. When the sentence was pronounced, Calvin asked that Servetus be given the more lenient sentence of death by beheading rather than being burned. He was refused, and Servetus was burned at the stake on 27 October 1553. From all this it seems absurd that Calvin should be held personally responsible. He was complicit in Servetus'

execution, it is true, but why should Calvin's reputation be so tar-
nished when the execution of Protestants and radicals by Catholics
and vice versa was a commonplace of the sixteenth century? All
Europe was agreed on Augustine's principle that heresy should
ultimately be dealt with by the secular sword. Unease with capital
punishment was simply not a feature of the times. Thus, if there was
a fault, it can be seen only as a fault of the age, not the man.

Two years after the Servetus affair, in 1555, the tide began to turn
for Calvin in Geneva. The council now began to be dominated by
his supporters, leaving him freer not only to reform Geneva, but
to turn it into an international centre for the propagation of the
gospel, especially in his native France. Calvin had already become
the inspiration and leader-in-exile of French Protestantism, writing
letters of support to churches as well as providing them with his
works of theology. Now, however, he could seriously set about the
evangelization of France. A secret programme was established to
infiltrate agents of the Reformation into France, using an under-
ground network, with safe houses and hiding places, so that pastors,
once trained in Geneva, could be slipped across the border to plant
covert new churches. Its success was astounding: the Reformed
faith exploded in numbers and influence in France. More than 10%
of the entire population became Reformed, as well as something
like a third of the nobility. The complete reformation of France
looked possible (that is, until 1572, after Calvin's death, when the
St Bartholomew's Day massacres of Protestants ended all such
hopes). But it was not only France: John Knox returned to Scotland
full of the vision of Geneva; English Protestants, who had fled
from Queen Mary's persecution, returned to bring the principles of
Geneva to Canterbury; missionaries were dispatched from Geneva
to Poland, Hungary, the Netherlands, Italy, even South America.
Geneva had become a nerve centre for world evangelization.

In 1559, to underpin all this mission and ministry, Calvin
opened a college and academy in Geneva, appointing Thèodore de
Bèze (or Beza) as rector. This was to provide a general education,
starting with classes in secondary studies, with theology as the
queen of the sciences. For the ripple effect it was to have on the
world, especially through the pastors trained there, the academy
was probably Calvin's crowning achievement.

On top of all this, Calvin preached and lectured almost daily and produced a steady stream of tracts, commentaries and revised editions of the *Institutes*. His contemporary Colladon wrote:

> Calvin for his part did not spare himself at all, working far beyond what his powers and regard for his health could stand. He preached commonly every day for one week in two. Every week he lectured three times in theology . . . He was at the *Consistoire* on the appointed day and made all the remonstrances. Every Friday at the Bible Study . . . what he added after the leader had made his *declaration* was almost a lecture. He never failed in visiting the sick, in private warning and counsel, and the rest of the numberless matters arising out of the ordinary exercise of his ministry. But besides these ordinary tasks, he had great care for believers in France, both in teaching them and exhorting and counselling them and consoling them by letters when they were being persecuted, and also in interceding for them, or getting another to intercede when he thought he saw an opening. Yet all that did not prevent him from going on working at his special study and composing many splendid and very useful books.[10]

All this was clearly to the detriment of his health, which declined to such an extent that he spent the last ten years of his life often in excruciating pain.[11] Yet he appears never to have taken a day off.

---

10. T. H. L. Parker, *Calvin's Preaching* (Louisville, Ky.: Westminster John Knox, 1992), pp. 62–63.

11. A few months before his death he wrote, 'at that time I was not attacked by arthritic pains, knew nothing of the stone or the gravel – I was not tormented with the gripings of the cholic, nor afflicted with hemorrhoids, nor threatened with expectoration of blood. At present all these ailments as it were in troops assail me. As soon as I recovered from a quartan ague, I was seized with severe and acute pains in the calves of my legs, which after being partially relieved returned a second and a third time. At last they degenerated into a disease in my articulations, which spread from my feet to my knees. An ulcer in the hemorrhoid veins long caused me excruciating sufferings, and intestinal ascarides subjected me to painful titillations, though I am now relieved from this vermicular disease, but immediately after in the course of last summer I had an attack of nephritis.

He died on 27 May 1564 and, according to his request, was buried in an unmarked grave so that in death he might not become a relic and so deny the Reformation he had lived for.

Calvin's thought

Calvin's theology was not original. Rather, it was 'fundamentally so old-fashioned that it seemed a novelty'.[12] Its brilliance lay instead in its clarity of exposition, its consistent rigour and orderly arrangement. Yet, because of its lack of originality, to understand Calvin best it is worth having a working knowledge of those theologies that

---

Footnote 11 (*cont.*)

As I could not endure the jolting motion of horseback, I was conveyed into the country in a litter. On my return I wished to accomplish a part of the journey on foot. I had scarcely proceeded a mile when I was obliged to repose myself, in consequence of lassitude in the reins. And then to my surprise I discovered that I discharged blood instead of urine. As soon as I got home I took to bed. The nephritis gave me exquisite pain, from which I only obtained a partial relief by the application of remedies. At length not without the most painful strainings I ejected a calculus which in some degree mitigated my sufferings, but such was its size, that it lacerated the urinary canal and a copious discharge of blood followed. This hemorrhage could only be arrested by an injection of milk through a syringe. After that I ejected several others, and the oppressive numbness of the reins is a sufficient symptom that there still exist there some remains of uric calculus. It is a fortunate thing, however, that minute or at least moderately sized particles still continue to be emitted. My sedentary way of life to which I am condemned by the gout in my feet precludes all hopes of a cure. I am also prevented from taking exercise on horseback by my hemorrhoids. Add to my other complaints that whatever nourishment I take imperfectly digested turns into phlegm, which by its density sticks like paste to my stomach' (Letter to the physicians of Montpellier, February 1564, *The Letters of John Calvin*, tr. Jules Bonnet [New York: Franklin, 1972], vol. 4, pp. 371–372).

12. Parker, *John Calvin*, p. 9.

influenced him most. Above all, two figures come to mind: Luther and Augustine. Luther's influence is more immediately obvious; but it is Augustine's name that appears more frequently than any other in Calvin's writings. In fact, it can hardly be said too strongly: to understand Calvin one must know Augustine.

That said, how might we best try to assimilate this phenomenon that is Calvin? In his 1541 Ecclesiastical Ordinances, four permanent church offices are mentioned: pastors, teachers or doctors, elders and deacons. Doctors are provided to teach the universal church (especially its pastors) and protect its doctrine; pastors teach a particular congregation, applying Scripture to them and administering the sacraments; elders are responsible for order and discipline; deacons provide for the social welfare of the people. Understanding these four offices not only serves to outline Calvin's view of how churches should operate; it also reveals how Calvin viewed the different aspects of his own ministry. Calvin believed that he had been given two offices: that of pastor and that of doctor/teacher. As a teacher he sought to teach the church, and especially its pastors, doctrine (which he did in the *Institutes*). This was done so as to understand Scripture (which he did in his commentaries and lectures). Thus he would equip pastors (including himself) who would then in turn teach the people doctrine (through the catechism) in order that they might understand Scripture better (which would happen primarily in sermons).[13] The *Institutes*, the commentaries, the catechism and the sermons thus serve as the four wheels of his ministry, and we can best acquaint ourselves with Calvin's thought by looking at each in turn.

The Institutes of the Christian Religion

It is his *Institutes*, however, that should take most of our time, for it is there that the distilled spirit of Calvin can be sampled. As such,

---

13. For a thorough unpacking of the relationship between these modules in his school of Christ, see Randall C. Zachman, *John Calvin as Teacher, Pastor and Theologian: The Shape of His Writings and Thought* (Grand Rapids: Baker, 2006).

it is an immensely rich and multifaceted work, and we must resist the popular temptation to reduce it to a single theme (the idea that Calvin was a theologian of one subject is usually attributed to him by those who would give him their own theme). What sort of work is the *Institutes*, then?

Calvin wrote the first, 1536, edition in refuge from the persecution of evangelicals in his native France. He dedicated it to Francis I, the king of France, arguing in the preface that accusations of heresy against them were unjustifiable, for they were following the true Christian religion that the king claimed to uphold as the legal religion of France. Such an apologia for the evangelical faith was vital not only for the authorities to read, but also for the evangelicals themselves, and thus was published as a physically small book, making it easy to be carried around (and hidden in a coat pocket when the time came for it to be banned).

It was much more than an apologia, however. The full title he gave the work was *Institutes of the Christian Religion Embracing Almost the Whole Sum of Piety, and whatever Is Necessary to Know of the Doctrine of Salvation: A Work Most Worthy to Be Read by All Persons Zealous for Piety, and Recently Published.* In Latin *Institutio* means 'instruction', and this was to be Calvin's chief aim. The work was thus structured on the framework of a traditional catechism as follows:

- Chapter 1: On the law (with an exposition of the Ten Commandments)
- Chapter 2: On faith (with an exposition of the Apostles' Creed)
- Chapter 3: On prayer (with an exposition of the Lord's Prayer)
- Chapter 4: On the sacraments

Two final chapters then deal polemically with issues of the day:

- Chapter 5: On the five 'false sacraments' of Roman Catholicism (confirmation, penance, extreme unction, ordination, marriage)
- Chapter 6: On the liberty of the Christian, ecclesiastical and civil government

He never understood this instruction in a merely cerebral way, however: his purpose, he wrote 'was solely to transmit certain rudiments by which those who are touched with any zeal for religion might be shaped to true godliness'.[14] It is this aim that falsifies the accusation that Calvin, being a theologian of the word and concerned with the knowledge of God, intellectualized faith. The *Institutes* is not a cold work to read. For true knowledge of God, as Calvin will make clear, is not something limited to the brain. 'How then is it possible for you to know God and yet be touched by no feeling?' he once asked.[15] Rather, Calvin wanted readers to feel the force of the truths under discussion so that their hearts might be won for Christ. He would speak repeatedly of God ravishing us with his love, wooing and inflaming our hearts with the knowledge of himself. This, he believed, was the point of doctrine: properly arranged and rightly taught, it is the most powerful force for real change deep in the hearts of real people.

Three years later, in the 1539 edition, Calvin substantially revised his creation. Rearranged, bulked up to seventeen chapters, at three times the size of the previous edition, the *Institutes* now had a more specific agenda: 'to prepare and train aspirants after sacred theology in reading the Divine Word'.[16] No longer just a catechism; here was a guide to Scripture. By this move the *Institutes* and Calvin's biblical commentaries could begin to work in tandem: with doctrine explained here, the commentaries could be dedicated to pure exegesis and kept from becoming overly long or cluttered by theological digressions. Two of his great concerns are thus revealed: first, he wanted his theology to be brief and simple, for he was interested in communicating theology rather than restricting it to specialists; secondly, he wanted the Bible to be read and understood by all so that the Christ of the Bible might be known by all. Both were in stark contrast to the withholding of the Bible from the people in medieval Roman Catholicism, and all of his efforts flowed from those concerns.

---

14. Epistle Dedicatory to Francis I, *Institutes of the Christian Religion, 1536 edition*, tr. F. L. Battles (Grand Rapids: Meeter Center & Eerdmans, 1975), p. 1.

15. Commentary on 1 John 2:3.

16. *Calvini Opera Selecta*, ed. P. Barth and W. Niesel (Munich: Kaiser, 1936), p. 255.

Calvin produced expanded and updated editions of the *Institutes* in 1543, 1545 and 1550. In 1559, however, he made his final and most radical revision. Now at about five times the size of the original, the material was arranged into four books. Not only does the new structure show how profoundly trinitarian Calvin's theology is; it also expresses his ongoing desire to show that the evangelical faith is simply creedal orthodoxy.

- Book 1: *The Knowledge of God the Creator* (corresponding to the first section of the Apostles' Creed, 'I believe in God the Father almighty')
- Book 2: *The Knowledge of God the Redeemer in Christ* (corresponding to the second section of the Apostles' Creed, 'I believe in Jesus Christ his only Son our Lord')
- Book 3: *The Way in which we Receive the Grace of Christ* (corresponding to the third section of the Apostles' Creed, 'I believe in the Holy Spirit'[17])
- Book 4: *The External Means or Aids by which God Invites us into the Society of Christ and Holds us therein* (corresponding to the section of the Apostles' Creed on 'the holy catholic Church')

Instead of making up a compendium of doctrines, the four books present a flowing argument that follows the proper development of a knowledge of God. In Book 1 we see that, while we have an innate awareness of divinity, we need enlightening by Scripture so as to distinguish the true God from all pretenders to true divinity. Then, in Book 2, we find that through knowing him we are made aware of our slavery to sin, and so are led to seek righteousness and wholeness in Christ. In Book 3, having been justified, we repent of our sinful ways, express our trust in God through prayer, and look with confidence to both our past (God's election of us) and future (the resurrection). Finally, in Book 4, we live out our

---

17. Though the person of the Spirit is not specifically dealt with, Calvin explains in the title of the first chapter of Book 3 that the things already spoken of concerning Christ (in Book 2) 'Profit Us by the Secret Working of the Spirit'.

JOHN CALVIN 53

faith in the world, enabled by the institutions of the church and the sacraments.

Such is the elegant structure of the 1559 edition. Now to some of the details that fill it.

Book 1: The Knowledge of God the Creator

'Nearly all the wisdom we possess, that is to say, true and sound wisdom, consists of two parts: the knowledge of God and of ourselves.' So Calvin begins and, in many ways, encapsulates the argument of the *Institutes*. The knowledge of God and ourselves are intertwined, he argues: man cannot know God until he knows himself as a sinner against God, his Creator. However, despite the fact that God's being is indelibly etched on all his creation, man ungratefully and culpably refuses to acknowledge him, and so remains a fool incapable of true wisdom. Thus 'whatever by ourselves we think concerning him [God] is foolish, and whatever we speak, absurd'.[18] It is as though by nature we were blind men in a theatre, unable to see or understand everything being communicated. Yet God graciously gives us the Scriptures to serve as spectacles, so that through them we might clearly perceive God, ourselves and all reality.

At this point Calvin needs to establish how these spectacles of Scripture have any authority. How can we trust them as being God's true revelation of reality? Calvin strongly denies that anyone or anything other than God (whether it be the church or our own reason) can authenticate God's Word to us. Thus 'they who strive to build up firm faith in Scripture through disputation are doing things backwards'.[19] Only God can do this, and he does so by his Spirit in Scripture itself:

> Scripture indeed is self-authenticated; hence, it is not right to subject it to proof and reasoning. And the certainty it deserves with us, it attains by the testimony of the Spirit. For even if it wins reverence for itself by its

---

18. *Institutes of the Christian Religion*, tr. F. L. Battles (Philadelphia: Westminster, 1960), 1.13.3. References to the *Institutes* consist of three numbers, identifying the book, chapter and section, respectively.

19. Ibid. 1.7.4.

own majesty, it seriously affects us only when it is sealed upon our hearts through the Spirit. Therefore, illumined by his power, we believe neither by our own nor by anyone else's judgment that Scripture is from God; but above human judgment we affirm with utter certainty (just as if we were gazing upon the majesty of God himself) that it has flowed to us from the very mouth of God by the ministry of men. We seek no proofs, no marks of genuineness upon which our judgment may lean; but we subject our judgment and wit to it as to a thing far beyond any guesswork![20]

This was to be essential to all Calvin's thought (and, indeed, all the Reformation). His theology was to have God's Word as its very deepest foundation, and he refused to smuggle in some other foundation or support for that, for then the entire edifice of his theology would be built upon the sand of human reason or tradition, rather than upon the solid rock of God's Word. That said, in the next chapter Calvin demonstrates that the belief we have come to in Scripture as God's Word is not misplaced, for there are reasonable evidences of its divine origin. This is not to contradict what he has already argued: these evidences could never foster belief; they are for the assurance of those who *already* believe.

Scripture, then, according to Calvin, is both indispensable and absolutely foundational for true godliness. However, exactly how he viewed the Bible is a hotly debated subject. What commentators are agreed on is that Calvin drew a very sharp distinction between God and man. God is infinite and spiritual; we are finite and material. As such, God must as it were use baby-talk when he speaks to us. 'Thus such forms of speaking do not so much express clearly what God is like as accommodate the knowledge of him to our slight capacity.'[21] The question that divides commentators is this: does this distinction between God-as-he-is and God-as-he-reveals-himself mean that there might be something misleading in his self-revelation? Or, to put it another way, might the sharpness of distinction between God and man mean that, for all the infallibility of God, a human author of Scripture might make a mistake?

---

20. Ibid. 1.7.5.
21. Ibid. 1.13.1.

Many – perhaps most – Calvin scholars today are happy to allow that Calvin thought so. Commonly cited are his comments on Acts 7:14, 16 (also Matt. 27:9), where he did say that there were errors in the text that ought to be amended. However, he seems to attribute them to later copyists. He does not ascribe error to Luke, but believed that the process of textual transmission could allow for minute and circumstantial error to creep in (more than that he could not allow, for he believed in the providential preservation of the Scriptures[22]). Such comments also need to be read within the context of his view that the Spirit, being concerned for all details great and small, literally dictated words to the human authors of Scripture 'as though he had said, "Let not a syllable be omitted, but let that which I once proclaimed by thy mouth, remain unchanged."'[23] The result for Calvin was the belief that in the Bible we hear 'the living words of God' as if 'having sprung from heaven'.[24] It is hard to imagine a much stronger affirmation of the complete inerrancy of Scripture.

To return to the argument, so far Calvin has shown that through Scripture we are taught the knowledge of the true God in distinction to all idols. He therefore spends the next chapters dealing with various forms of idolatry. The true God, he then argues, is most clearly distinguished from all idols by the fact that when we encounter the one living God, we encounter three persons. Indeed, unless when we consider the one God we think of the three persons, 'only the bare and empty name of God flits about in our brains, to the exclusion of the true God'.[25] Here Calvin feels the need to depart from Augustine, since he is critical of Augustine's use of analogies for understanding the Trinity (though, out of affection, he desists from naming and shaming his hero).[26] Calvin prefers instead to look to the Old and New

---

22. Ibid. 1.6.3; 1.8.9–10.
23. Commentary on Jeremiah 36:28; cf. comments on Jer.36:4–8; 2 Tim. 3:16; *Institutes* 1.18.3; 3.25.8; 4.8.6, 9.
24. *Institutes* 1.7.1.
25. Ibid. 1.13.2.
26. Ibid. 1.13.18.

Testaments to understand the relationships that exist between the Father, Son and Spirit. He then uses Scripture to deal with various trinitarian heresies that were problematic at the time.

From chapter 14 Calvin moves on to the work of the triune Creator, his providential rule and relation to humans and angels. However, the chapters on God's providence that most readers have been anticipating from Calvin show none of the cold tone commonly expected. He states instead that God's work as Creator is not understood unless it includes an understanding of God's all-encompassing fatherly guidance of his creation. This providence is nothing like fate or chance; it is God's personal, ongoing kindness that brings the believer an otherwise unattainable comfort in this world of dangers. This is especially true of God's guidance in what appears to be accidental or out of control evil:

> When dense clouds darken the sky, and a violent tempest arises, because a gloomy mist is cast over our eyes, thunder strikes our ears and all our senses are benumbed with fright, everything seems to us to be confused and mixed up; but all the while a constant quiet and serenity ever remain in heaven. So must we infer that, while the disturbances in the world deprive us of judgment, God out of the pure light of his justice and wisdom tempers and directs these very movements in the best-conceived order to a right end.[27]

Does this make God the author of evil? Calvin takes the example of Judas and the answer of Augustine: when Judas sinned in handing over Jesus, why was the Father not considered equally guilty for handing over his Son? Because by it Judas meant evil and the Father good.[28]

Book 2: The Knowledge of God the Redeemer in Christ

Having shown how the knowledge of God is revealed in the Scriptures, Calvin now explains what we learn there about ourselves. That is, Adam became a sinner by refusing to trust God's

27. Ibid. 1.17.1.
28. Ibid. 1.18.4.

word; he then propagated from himself a race of sinners born with his guilty status and sinful nature. As such, we find that we are all sinners, not by imitation, but by birth; and not merely empty of good, but full of evil. Our wills are instinctively bent towards evil faithlessness so that we always choose evil and find ourselves incapable of doing anything good. This, Calvin argues forcefully, is the testimony of both Scripture and the church fathers, that we are by nature helplessly enslaved to sin. Thus we see our desperate need for redemption.

That redemption is found in Christ alone, as it always has been from the beginning of the world, for 'apart from the Mediator, God never showed favor toward the ancient people, nor ever gave hope of grace to them . . . [so that] the hope of all the godly has ever reposed in Christ alone'.[29] Thus, he argues, true faith always has been and always will be faith in Christ. This was why the law of Moses was given, full of visual aids proclaiming Christ's work, so that, being made aware of their sin, the people might seek the Redeemer. The law would then sustain them in the obedience of faith, restraining them from evil and from becoming careless about righteousness, and giving them instruction about the Lord's will and pleasure.

This leads Calvin into an examination of the relationship between the Old and New Testaments. His view is simple: they are exactly the same in their substance, and differ only in administration. To help the reader understand this, he provides three principles for correctly understanding the Old Testament: first, the Jews were given not merely earthly blessings but everlasting hopes; secondly, the covenant was one of mercy, not works; thirdly, 'they had and knew Christ as Mediator, through whom they were joined to God and were to share in his promises'.[30]

After this essential excursion we see how Christ redeems. He begins with the incarnation, how Christ assumed our flesh without sin so as to take what was ours (guilt and death) and give what was his (righteousness and life). So far this sounds

---

29. Ibid. 2.6.2–3; cf. 4.8.5.
30. Ibid. 2.10.2.

historically conventional; however, Calvin's next point quickly became perhaps the most fundamental point of disagreement between Lutherans and Calvinists.[31] Calvin argues that while the Word truly became flesh, the Word was not limited to the man, Jesus. When Jesus was in Mary's womb, the Word also remained outside Jesus in heaven. Lutherans objected that this 'Calvinist extra' was a denial of Colossians 2:9, and made Christ a separate being behind and outside Jesus. Yet for Calvin this was not a point to be conceded lightly: it entailed a complete understanding of what God is like and how he reveals himself. Just as God cannot reveal himself to us entirely when he speaks, but must accommodate his revelation to our weak capacity, so the Word cannot give himself entirely to us. Just as there is a distinction between God-as-he-is and God-as-he-reveals-himself, so there must be a distinction between the Word as he is and the man, Jesus.

Next Calvin explains how Christ is prophet, priest and king. He was anointed to these three offices by the Holy Spirit for the sake of his body, the church, so that not only might we enjoy his prophetic revelation, his priestly mediation and his kingly rule, but also, filled with the Spirit of his anointing, we might be prophets, priests interceding and offering sacrifices of prayer and praise, and kings ruling over sin, death and the devil. Not only remarkably comprehensive for its brevity, it also remains one of the most powerful arguments for the replacement of the Roman sacerdotal priesthood with the priesthood of all believers.

Finally, he turns to see how we who are dead can find life through the death, resurrection and ascension of Christ. Our problem, he emphasizes, is God's wrath at sin. Yet (and here he quotes Augustine) 'in a marvelous and divine way he loved us

----

31. The differences, in fact, were not at all new: Lutheranism was in many ways the child of the ancient school of theology in Alexandria (which emphasized the unity of God and man in Christ), while Calvinism was much more closely aligned with the theological school of Antioch (which emphasized the distinction between divinity and humanity).

even when he hated us'.³² So, through the obedience of Christ, this
became our acquittal:

> the guilt that held us liable for punishment has been transferred to the
> head of the Son of God. We must, above all, remember this substitution,
> lest we tremble and remain anxious throughout life – as if God's
> righteous vengeance, which the Son of God has taken upon himself, still
> hung over us.³³

Having defeated hell on the cross, Christ was then raised up to
give us life before entering heaven 'in our name'.³⁴ That he will
return in judgment Calvin shows is a comfort for believers who
know and love the Judge. Christ's person and work having then
been presented, Calvin finishes the book by exhorting readers to
seek their every blessing in Christ.

Book 3: The Way in which we Receive the Grace of Christ

The way in which Calvin now moves the argument on is explained
in the title of chapter 1: 'The Things which Have Been Said about
Christ Profit us by the Secret Activity of the Spirit.' That is, by the
Spirit we are united to Christ so as to enjoy all he has done for us.

The Spirit's first work, he says, is to create in us faith, which
Calvin then defines. True faith is not an opinion or a mere assent
that the gospel is true, nor is it belief in 'God' in general. Rather,
as argued before, true faith always has been and always will be
specifically faith in Christ. In fact, true faith can only be defined
in a trinitarian way, as 'a firm and certain knowledge of God's
benevolence toward us, founded upon the truth of the freely given
promise in Christ, both revealed to our minds and sealed upon our
hearts through the Holy Spirit'.³⁵ As such, true faith is unwavering.
This is not to suggest that the true believer has no doubts, but that
'at heart believers are on the side of their faith and its object in

---

32. *Institutes* 2.16.4.
33. Ibid. 2.16.5.
34. Ibid. 2.16.16.
35. Ibid. 3.2.7.

opposition to their doubts and temptations'.[36] In faith we 'prick up
the ears [to God's Word] and close the eyes [to the doubt-causing
lies of the world, the flesh and the devil]'.[37]

True faith is, fundamentally, something of the heart, not merely
an act of the brain acknowledging truth. For this reason true faith is
inseparable from love to God. Calvin therefore moves to speak of
the repentance (or 'regeneration', as he puts it) that flows from faith.
Repentance must originate in faith, for it is impossible to be truly
conscious of sin without faith; it then reaches its goal in such a self-
denying, total submission to God's good pleasure that one is never
miserable with one's lot. A happy definition of repentance indeed!

Only after covering the life of repentance and sanctification
does Calvin return to look at justification by faith alone. He
seems to have proceeded in this unusual order to pre-empt the
Roman Catholic criticism that justification by faith alone leaves a
Christianity devoid of Christian living (it is not that Calvin is weak
on justification – this section, chs. 11–19, is one of the longest
in the *Institutes*). At heart, justification, he explains, consists of
Christ's righteousness being imputed to the sinner. He uses an
illustration of Ambrose's to explain: in order to receive a blessing
from his father, Jacob approached him while wearing the clothes
of his firstborn brother, Esau. Just so, to be blessed by God
the Father, sinners approach him, not on the basis of any righteousness in their own lives, but by clothing themselves with the
righteousness of the firstborn, Christ.[38]

This justification is understood properly only if it entails a real
belief in the Christian's freedom, which he explains next. One
quotation from this chapter should suffice to break the image of
Calvin the pernickety moralist:

> when consciences once ensnare themselves, they enter a long and
> inextricable maze, not easy to get out of. If a man begins to doubt

---

36. T. H. L. Parker, *Calvin: An Introduction to His Thought* (Louisville, Ky.:
    Westminster John Knox, 1995), p. 82.

37. *Institutes* 3.13.14.

38. Ibid. 3.11.23.

whether he may use linen for sheets, shirts, handkerchiefs, and napkins, he will afterward be uncertain also about hemp; finally, doubt will even arise over tow. For he will turn over in his mind whether he can sup without napkins, or go without a handkerchief. If any man should consider daintier food unlawful, in the end he will not be at peace before God, when he eats either black bread or common victuals, while it occurs to him that he could sustain his body on even coarser foods. If he boggles at sweet wine, he will not with clear conscience drink even flat wine, and finally he will not dare touch water if sweeter and cleaner than other water.[39]

He comes next to prayer, the 'chief exercise of faith'. Faith is that wise recognition of our own lack and of Christ's fullness of grace. Prayer puts that recognition into action. Furthermore, prayer not only recognizes Christ's riches; it must know him as mediator: the thought of God's majesty naturally makes us shrink from prayer, and we are capable of approaching the living God with boldness only when we remember and depend upon Christ. Pastorally concerned as ever, Calvin proceeds to give practical advice and encouragement in this chief exercise.

It is only now (on p. 920 of the standard F. L. Battles edition of the *Institutes*!), and briefly, that Calvin comes to deal with the doctrine for which he is most famous: election. As an integral part of his overall pastoral argument, Calvin presents election not as a doctrine of fear but as one of comfort in that it proclaims God's absolute and free mercy. That is, God, in his free pleasure, rather than on the basis of anything in individuals, chooses to predestine some to salvation and others to damnation. Yet, Calvin argues, election is not primarily an individualistic thing: it is about being destined by God to be engrafted into Christ. Thus all grounds for confidence and salvation are found in him, not in ourselves. In Christ the elect are eternally secure and cannot fall away. As for God's rejection of sinners, Calvin strongly maintains that this is entirely just (God could not act otherwise). Sinners deserve to be rejected, and God has chosen not to be merciful to some so as to magnify his own glory.

---

39. Ibid. 3.19.7.

From the eternity past of God's election Calvin next takes us
to the end of all things: the universal bodily resurrection. Christ's
bodily resurrection is shared by his body, the church, and all things
over which he is Head, thus accounting for the resurrection of
unbelievers to judgment.

Book 4: The External Means or Aids by which God Invites us into the Society of Christ and Holds us therein

Following the Reformation break with Rome, the credible sur-
vival of Protestantism depended on the ability of the Reformers
to produce a robust ecclesiology. If Rome really was the one
true church, then Protestants were just schismatics. It was Calvin
above all who rose to the challenge, by dedicating the final quarter
of his *Institutes* to providing the most comprehensive and definitive
ecclesiology of the Reformation.

Instead of shying away from a high view of the church, Calvin
agreed with Rome's Augustinian principle that the church is the
necessary mother of all believers. He disagreed with the separatist
dream that the church in this age could ever be perfect. Instead, he
believed, the true church could be recognized, not by its allegiance
to the pope, nor by its perfect separation from the world, but by
two marks: 'Wherever we see the Word of God purely preached
and heard, and the sacraments administered according to Christ's
institution, there, it is not to be doubted, a church of God exists.'[40]
That is, Christ governs his body through his Word in both proclamation and sign; in contrast, in the false church of the pope,
there Christ does not rule through his Word, meaning that there
the church has lost connection with its Head and is like a man
with his throat cut. Thus, while Rome accused the Reformers of
schism, Calvin, by his definition of the church, turned the tables to
accuse Rome of schism.

Calvin then moves with telling speed to speak of the ministers

---

40. Ibid. 4.1.9. Reformed theology after Calvin tended to make discipline a
    third mark of the church. Calvin did not do so, though that is not to say
    he would have disagreed: he certainly spoke strongly of the necessity of
    church discipline (*Institutes* 4.12.1) and sought to enforce it in Geneva.

of God's Word in his church. They are the vital sinews that hold the body together, for through them the word that constitutes the church is ministered. He held that Ephesians 4:11 taught that there are five sorts of ministers: apostles, prophets, evangelists, pastors, teachers. The first three he saw as temporary offices that had generally ceased (though he believed that God still uses them in extraordinary circumstances, Luther having been just such an extraordinary apostle). The offices of pastor and teacher have been explained above. In case any misunderstand Calvin to be sending the church back to Roman Catholic structuralism, by simply replacing bishops with preachers, he then (after a largely historical analysis of the claims of Rome) examines the question of authority in the Church. Authority, he argues, resides not with the ministers per se, but only in God's Word, which they are to minister.

What then of the sacraments? They too are about the preaching of the gospel in that they confirm and present it by external signs.[41] In contrast to Zwingli, Calvin did not believe that sacraments are essentially oaths of our allegiance to Christ. Primarily, they are from God to us: they truly present and offer us the blessings of the gospel. Yet that is not to agree with Rome's sacramentalism: sacraments have no inherent power to bestow grace, but are efficacious only in so far as they are used by the Spirit.

While many different sacraments were given in the Old Testament to lead people to Christ, now just two flow from him to us: the water and the blood. Baptism, corresponding to circumcision, presents initiation into Christ with all its benefits. Calvin is quite relaxed about questions of immersion and sprinkling; he is, however, prepared to argue at some length that infant baptism accords best with the nature of the sacrament. The Lord's Supper is the next sacrament, for the nourishment of those who have been baptized into Christ. In it we are invited to feed on the body and blood of Christ crucified.[42]

---

41. Ibid. 4.14.1.
42. Unfortunately, there is simply not the space here to examine the important question of how Calvin distinguished his understanding of the Lord's Supper from that of Zwingli, Luther and Rome. For a brief but

Calvin's great work then ends on what might seem like an anti-climax: a chapter on civil government. Yet it is a quite proper end point for him, since true knowledge of God, once received, must then be lived out in the world. Calvin carefully maps out his position in contrast to the many political views of the magisterial and radical Reformations: he refuses to follow the Zwinglian confusion of church and state; he avoids the Lutheran submission of church to state; Anabaptist separatism, he holds, forgets that we still live in these bodies in this age; radical revolution confuses Christian liberty with the removal of political hierarchy. Instead, political powers exist to protect and prosper the work of the Word through the church. Yet even when they do not, and they become unjust, Christians are enjoined to civil obedience. Calvin has one qualification, on which he appropriately, if somewhat abruptly, ends: that our first and overriding obedience is always to God.

Commentaries

Through the *Institutes* Calvin provided a guide to Scripture; the other half of his doctoral office involved the plain exposition of the Scriptures. In this way he sought to avoid both the imposition of doctrine onto texts and the study of doctrines in abstraction from their place in the story of Scripture.

Calvin managed to expound almost every book of the Bible. Yet most of what we think of as Calvin's commentaries are in fact transcripts of expository lectures given to Genevan schoolboys and ministers. They were delivered in Latin, with Greek and Hebrew being used and analysed. To the relief of the students, Calvin's breathing difficulties meant that all this happened extremely slowly!

In his exegesis, as elsewhere, Calvin was concerned to remain

---

Footnote 42 (*cont.*)

extremely helpful introduction to this, see F. Wendel, *Calvin: The Origins and Development of his Religious Thought* (London: Collins, 1963), ch. 5, pt. 4, pp. 329–355.

within the orthodox tradition; however, it is here that Calvin's humanist training shows through most clearly, making him a true pioneer. He did not share Luther's paramount determination to see how each page of Scripture proclaims Christ; his overriding concern was to find each passage's original, simple, grammatical meaning, and then to convey it equally simply. For this, he believed, context was essential, context being not only a passage's place in the overall text, but also its linguistic context (how matters are expressed in the language in which the passage was written) and historical context (for which he was keen to use as much extra-biblical material as possible). The result is that Calvin's commentaries look distinctly modern.

Catechism

For Calvin, doctrine is too useful to be restricted to books: it must be put into the hands, hearts and minds of every Christian. Thus, in 1538, shifting from his doctoral to his pastoral role, he boiled down the first edition of his *Institutes* to make a catechism for the people, especially the children. In 1545 he revised this to create the Geneva Catechism, which was to have an important role in the spread of the Reformed faith, and became the basis for the Heidelberg Catechism, the primary Reformed catechism. The catechism consists of five sections: on faith, then law (significantly reversing Luther's order), prayer, the Word, the sacraments. Through this, children in Geneva – unlike those in Rome – were encouraged to investigate their faith. They were compelled to consider what they believed and why, to know the benefits of their belief, and to have ready arguments against, for example, Rome's denial of justification by faith alone or the Anabaptist denial of infant baptism. The result was that the Reformed faith was to have resilient grassroots.

Sermons

Calvin is rarely thought of as a preacher, yet, when standing in his pulpit, his leading biographer, Émile Doumergue, exclaimed,

'That is the Calvin who seems to me to be the real and authentic Calvin, the one who explains all the others: Calvin the preacher of Geneva.'[43] Certainly, he spent much of his time in Geneva preaching: twice on Sundays (New Testament) and, on alternate weeks, every weekday as well (Old Testament), each time for about an hour.

His sermons were transcribed for us to read, but he had no manuscript himself; instead, he would study his text for a day, walk straight from his study to the pulpit and preach directly from the Hebrew or Greek (without any anecdotes or 'display'). His lack of notes gave his sermons a much more popular feel than his lectures, a feel he deliberately cultivated as he removed all specialist language and technical material. He did not cite any Greek, Hebrew or Latin, but spoke a plain, everyday French (though with a little less ease than Luther spoke the earthy German of the people). Yet he treated his listeners as real students of the Bible, and assumed they had also been reading it for themselves. And undoubtedly their biblical literacy would have been high as, week by week and verse by verse, he worked through entire books of the Bible with them.

This surely is the authentic Calvin who explains all the others, for his entire life's work was to open and convey the Word of God so that the people might be won, heart and mind, to true knowledge of God.

Going on with Calvin

Calvin usually surprises first-time readers with his warmth and accessibility. Nobody who has survived this introduction will have any trouble reading and enjoying the *Institutes*, and that should be where to go from here. The Ford Lewis Battles two-volume translation of the 1559 edition (Philadelphia: Westminster Press, 1960) is undoubtedly the standard and best: quite apart from the quality

---

43. Quoted by L. Nixon, *John Calvin, Expository Preacher* (Grand Rapids: Eerdmans, 1950), p. 38.

of translation, it has excellent footnotes and indices that make it markedly superior to the old nineteenth-century Beveridge translation. John Dillenberger's anthology *John Calvin: Selections from His Writings* (New York: Anchor, 1971) provides a good collection of some of Calvin's other works.

Readers need to be more careful with biographies and secondary literature on Calvin: many are highly opinionated and biased. François Wendel's *Calvin: The Origins and Development of his Religious Thought* (London: Collins, 1963) is the classic single-volume introduction to the man and his thought. After that, try anything by T. H. L. Parker, who has written first-rate books on the man, the *Institutes*, his commentaries and his preaching.

If you start the journey, you should soon find that, like Karl Barth, you could gladly and profitably set yourself down and spend at least some of your life just with Calvin.

John Calvin timeline[44]

1509	Calvin born in Noyon, France
1520–21?	Theological studies at the University of Paris
1525–6?	Moved to study law at the University of Orléans
1529–30?	Studies at the University of Bourges; converted
1534?	Flees Paris
1535?	Arrives in Basel
1536	First edition of the *Institutes* is published; he arrives in Geneva
1537	Submits *Articles on the Organization of the Church and its Worship at Geneva* to council
1538	Expelled from Geneva; he settles in Strasbourg with Bucer
1539	Second edition of the *Institutes*
1540	Marries Idelette de Bure
1541	Returns to Geneva; submits Ecclesiastical Ordinances to council
1543, 1545	New editions of the *Institutes*
1549	Idelette dies
1550	Fifth edition of the *Institutes*
1553	Michael Servetus arrested and burned
1559	Final edition of the *Institutes*; college and academy opened
1564	Calvin dies

---

44. Some of the early dates of Calvin's life, especially those of his studies
    and conversion, are uncertain. The date of his conversion is especially
    disputed, being placed anywhere between 1527 and 1534. I have followed
    the revisionist chronology of T. H. L. Parker, who has been most rigorous
    in sifting the documentary evidence ('Arguments for Re-dating', in *John
    Calvin: A Biography* [Oxford: Lion, 2006], pp. 192–198).

3. LET US SEEK HEAVEN

John Owen

For some reason, Britain has never been a great breeding ground for theologians. Perhaps it is the pragmatism of the national spirit that stifles things; perhaps the curse of the Welshman, Pelagius, lies on the land. In any case, after him one struggles to think of many theologians who are both pre-eminent and British. The prize of being Britain's greatest-ever theologian may, then, be relatively uncontested, but one of the hottest candidates is probably John Owen. Once dubbed 'the Calvin of England', he was elephantine in almost every way.

Owen's life

In 1616, the year William Shakespeare died, John Owen was born into a Puritan parsonage and a country seething with religious and political tension. Of course, growing up in the little village of Stadham (now Stadhampton), outside Oxford, it would be a few years before he really felt that tension for himself.

At twelve years of age he entered Queen's College, Oxford. To

start student life so young is what surprises us, but what was actually exceptional for the time was the manic intensity with which
he drove himself to work. Allowing himself just four hours' sleep
a night, he wracked his health so that he might learn faster. He
sought to refresh himself especially through flute-playing, javelin-
flinging and long-jumping, but his relentless timetable would take
its toll in the years to come.

Aged nineteen he received his MA and was ordained, but in the
1630s 'high church' Oxford was no place for a young pastor with
Owen's Puritan convictions. He decided to take some household
chaplaincy jobs: there in private homes he could minister and
study unmolested by a church hierarchy increasingly intolerant of
his views.

All this time he was sinking ever deeper into depression and
self-isolation. Having spent his whole life in Puritan circles, he was
acutely conscious of his sin, but knew nothing of the assurance of
salvation that some preached. Then, in 1642, he moved to London
and went to hear a renowned preacher, Edmund Calamy, in St
Mary's Church, Aldermanbury. As it turned out, however, Calamy
was not there that day, and an unknown preacher was in the pulpit
instead. He took Matthew 8:26 as his text, 'Why are ye fearful, O
ye of little faith?' (Authorized Version). And with that message
Owen felt an immediate assurance that he had been born again of
the Spirit and was a child of God.

Even before that great personal turning point, Owen had started
on his first book, a work entitled *A Display of Arminianism*. There
was nothing particularly special about it – it was really the polemic
of a young man seeking to make his mark – but it laid out a basic
theological position Owen would always hold. Owen believed
passionately in the 'five points of Calvinism',[1] and Arminianism,

1. The 'five points of Calvinism', agreed at the Synod of Dordt in 1618–19,
   affirm (1) *Total Depravity* (meaning, not that we are as sinful as we possibly
   could be, but that sin has so comprehensively affected us that we have no
   ability to do anything towards our own salvation); (2) *Unconditional Election*
   (meaning that God unconditionally chooses some people for salvation
   and others for damnation, and does not base that decision on anything

which denied those five points, he viewed as a disturbing heresy
that opened the door to the worst denials of the gospel. In the
years to come he would pen lengthy defences of limited atonement (*The Death of Death in the Death of Christ*) and the perseverance
of the saints (*The Doctrine of the Saints' Perseverance Explained and
Confirmed*). For now, *A Display of Arminianism* focused on total
depravity, predestination and the irresistibility of God's grace.

It might seem strange that Owen, who, not long before, had left
Oxford because of his views, should now consider such polem-
ical theology to be career advancing. But by this time civil war had
broken out between the largely 'high church' party of King Charles
I and the predominantly Puritan forces of Parliament. And to the
Parliamentarians *A Display of Arminianism* was, indeed, welcome.
They made him vicar of Fordham, a village just outside Colchester.

Fordham gave Owen plenty to do. The previous incumbent
had been an ardent high churchman, and so the parishioners had
received no evangelical teaching. Thus, on top of his ordinary
duties, Owen composed a catechism for adults and a catechism for
children and went about the village instructing them. What with
the time he still had for his own writing, the Fordham years seem
to have been some of Owen's very happiest. And it was there that
he met and married Mary Rooke. That surely added to the happiness in Fordham. But the next thirty years of their marriage would
be scarred by pain: Mary bore John eleven children, all of whom
died before him, only one even surviving to adulthood.

After three short years, circumstances forced him to move to
minister in nearby Coggeshall. It was becoming quite obvious
now that Owen was a rising star (in 1646 he was asked to preach
before the House of Commons in Westminster) and the people of
Coggeshall, who had become gourmands of evangelical preaching,

---

within those people, whether good or bad); (3) *Limited Atonement* (meaning
that, on the cross, Christ paid for the sins of the elect only, not for the sins
of all humanity); (4) *Irresistible Grace* (meaning that, when God intends to
save a person, that person will be unable to resist and refuse to be born
again); and (5) the *Perseverance of the Saints* (meaning that God preserves
true Christians to the end, never letting them 'fall away' from salvation).

were eager to have Owen in their pulpit. Every Sunday some two thousand people now crowded into the church to hear him.

Then, on 30 January 1649, King Charles was executed, along with the hopes of the 'high church' party. It is testimony to Owen's newly acquired national stature that he was the one asked to preach to Parliament the next day. And what he said was highly revealing. Clearly, he was excited at what he saw happening in England. He believed it had all been prophesied as God's plan for the last days: with the execution of the king and the defeat of his tyranny, the reign of the antichrist was coming to an end, and with his destruction a triumphant millennial age for the church was being ushered in. Now the gospel could be proclaimed without hindrance, the church could be reformed and Christ would fill the world with light and love. It was an optimistic, millenarian vision that more and more were flocking to.

Owen's message certainly sat well with Parliament. He was invited to preach to them again, and this time was heard by Oliver Cromwell, the general of the Parliamentarian army and a man deeply interested in prophecy and how the cause of Parliament was the prophesied cause of God. Cromwell was just preparing to leave for Ireland to subdue a Catholic uprising there and asked Owen to come along as his chaplain.

The next couple of years thus saw Owen as Cromwell's chaplain, first in Ireland (where he hoped to turn Trinity College, Dublin, into a seminary of gospel preachers), and then in Scotland, where Cromwell's army turned next. But that role was really just a stepping stone to the big opportunity won for him by Cromwell's victories: in 1651 he was appointed Dean of Christ Church, Oxford, and, a year later, Vice-Chancellor of Oxford University.

The fact that Owen could be appointed Vice-Chancellor shows how much England had changed since he had left Oxford fifteen years earlier. And Oxford itself had changed: many of the 'high church' old guard had been replaced by Puritans from Cambridge. There was much still to be done, but Owen was positive that Oxford and Cambridge could be turned into the seedbeds of England's gospel renewal. What was needed was for a generation of young scholars and preachers to be educated in the gospel; they would then go out to educate the nation. As a result, Owen saw his principle duties as Vice-Chancellor being preaching and teaching. In addition to his lectures and occasional sermons around Oxford, he made sure that he preached at the University Church of St Mary's every second Sunday (one series becoming perhaps his most popular devotional work, *On the Mortification of Sin*).

In many ways they were golden years in Oxford: the university was transformed and Owen enjoyed the work. Of course, it helped that he earned something like ten times the average pastor's wage. But then it was for just such reasons that he began to be criticized by fellow Puritans. The money he spent in his preference for fine clothes and Spanish leather boots rather than academic garb attracted much vitriol. One censor (from Cambridge) complained that Oxford's Vice-Chancellor had 'as much powder in his hair as would discharge eight cannons'. Others complained that he was abandoning the local church.

In 1657 Owen felt it right to hand on the office of Vice-Chancellor, and from that moment he drifted out of the national spotlight. His great patron, Oliver Cromwell, died the next year, and the balance of political power fell, once again, into the hands of his antagonists. For more than ten years Owen had been a Congregationalist in his view of the church (i.e. he believed that each local church should be independent), and Cromwell's agreement with Owen gave protection to what was otherwise a minority position. But with Cromwell's death, the Presbyterians (who believed that local churches should be governed in groups by 'presbyteries' or meetings of assembled elders) gained the upper hand and Congregationalists like Owen started to be sidelined. The Congregationalists quickly arranged a conference to be held at the Savoy Palace in London, and produced a *Declaration of Faith and Order* 'to clear ourselves of that scandal which not only some persons at home but of foreign parts have affixed on us, viz. That Independentism [Congregationalism] is the sink of all heresies and schisms'.[2] But the tide was irreversible and Owen was left to a quiet retirement back in Stadham.

---

2. *The Savoy Declaration of Faith and Order*, ed. A. G. Matthews (London: Independent, 1959), p. 12.

At least it gave him time to write. Tucked away in rural Oxfordshire he managed to produce his monumental Latin treatise *Theologoumena Pantodapa* (Theological Statements of All Sorts), a grand history of theology from the time of Adam, including a look at the growth of idolatry in the nations, true theology in Israel, right on down to the practice of theology in his day.[3]

Those easy days were not to last, though, for in 1660 the beheaded king's son returned from exile and was crowned Charles II. Prospects were not good for a former chaplain to Cromwell, and life over the years that followed was made increasingly difficult for those, like Owen, now outside the Church of England. Before long, his house was raided by the militia and he was caught and prosecuted for preaching to some thirty people (religious assemblies of more than five people outside the parish church having been made illegal).

He considered emigrating (and there were universities and churches in Holland and New England that were eager to have him). Eventually, though, he decided to stay, to keep preaching and to campaign for toleration to be shown to non-Anglicans like himself. Given his status as a leading Congregationalist theologian, it was important for English Nonconformism that he did stay: where he went, others would follow. And he had connections that could help them, as his Congregationalist friend John Bunyan found out. Owen could not keep him out of prison for his preaching, but he could find him a publisher for his new book, *Pilgrim's Progress.*

For Owen in these later, more harassed years, the nature of the church became a major concern in his writings. He wanted more than toleration; he wanted to show that the Congregational way is the biblical way. But these writings reveal something more fundamental than Owen's view of how the church should operate: they

---

3. While it was originally included in Goold's nineteenth-century collection of Owen's works, Banner of Truth cut all Owen's Latin writings from their edition. However, *Theologoumena Pantodapa* has now been translated and published under the title *Biblical Theology*, tr. Stephen P. Westcott (Morgan, Pa.: Soli Deo Gloria, 1994).

express his very understanding of reformation. For Owen, reformation was essentially about separation from the ungodly. 'Come out from among them' was the sort of phrase heard much in his sermons.

Owen moved to London to pastor a church there while continuing to produce major works of theology. The London years saw such mature pieces as his massive commentary on Hebrews, *Pneumatologia*, *The Doctrine of Justification by Faith* and *Christologia*. If one knew no more, Owen would sound like just another harmless theologian. There was, however, a secret side to Owen's life. Behind closed doors he dabbled in radical politics: he seems to have been in on a plot to assassinate Charles II and place the Protestant Duke of Monmouth on the throne; government spies monitored his activity, considering him a threat; and once, when his house was searched, six or seven cases of pistols were discovered. Not the sort of thing found in the homes of respectable academic theologians!

In 1675 Mary, his wife for a little over thirty years, died. Not having his personal journals, we can only imagine how he reacted. But within eighteen months he was married again, this time to Dorothy D'Oyley. Owen was now sixty years old, and there were no children from this second marriage. Six years later, the one daughter (from the first marriage) who had made it to adulthood died. A year after that, Owen himself fell terminally ill, and on 24 August 1683 died in the quiet village of Ealing, outside London. Had he survived another six years he would have lived to see the religious liberty he had fought for granted in the Toleration Act of 1689.

Owen's thought

Death seemed unable to take Owen quickly, something ascribed by his doctor to 'the strength of his brain'. Whatever exactly that meant to a seventeenth-century physician, Owen's brain was strong. He did not have the piercing brilliance of an Athanasius or a Luther. Owen was much more ponderous. However, there was a breadth to his intellect that invited grand projects, meshing linguistic skill and doctrinal sensibility, biblical exegesis and historical theology.

As such, he was more than a theologian of one theme. He had a particular concern for high Calvinist and Congregationalist theology, but his interests ranged much more widely, as his personal reading, as much as his writing, attests: his library contained books on almost everything from classical literature and language to music, magic and home-brewing.

However, while he did not have one pet theme, he did bring to the theology of the day his own particular flavour. Even putting it so mildly could be misleading, for perhaps more than anything else that flavour is trinitarianism, and it would be absurd to call that Owen's own. And yet Owen's thought was so entirely moulded by the Trinity that trinitarianism became a (possibly *the*) driving characteristic of his theology. He believed that knowledge of God's triune being should shape all Christian belief and practice. Of course, all Christians nod along in agreement, but for Owen this actually made a profound difference. Owen's theology has been divided up and arranged in various ways, but he himself believed that God's triune being places all studies of his ways under one of two governing 'heads': Christology, which deals with God's giving of his Son; and pneumatology, which deals with God's giving of his Spirit.

Owen never wrote a systematic theology, and so probably the best way to get under his theological skin is to focus on those works where he deals with the doctrines he believed shape all true theology: *Communion with God, Christologia* and *Pneumatologia*.

Communion with God

Communion with God the Father, Son and Holy Ghost, Each Person Distinctly, in Love, Grace, and Consolation (!) was published shortly after Owen stepped down as Vice-Chancellor of Oxford University, but probably grew out of sermons he had given back in Coggeshall. Perhaps more than any other work, it captures Owen's heartbeat for theology to be both resolutely trinitarian and thoroughly applied. Essentially, it is a summons for Christians to be trinitarian in practice.

Owen was emphatic that it is quite impossible for anyone ever to have anything to do with 'God', simply put. There is no undifferentiated Godhead for any to deal with:

> And those who in their worship or invocation do attempt an approach unto the divine nature as absolutely considered, without respect unto the dispensation of God in the distinct persons of the holy Trinity, do reject the mystery of the Gospel, and all the benefit of it. So is it with many.[4]

Rather, Christians worship each person distinctly. That is not to say we imagine one person is separable from the others (we can only, for example, worship the Son as the Son of the Father, meaning that when we worship the Son aright, we worship the Father who begets him and the Spirit who unites us to him). But the Father, Son and Spirit are distinct persons, and Owen wants to show how we have distinct communion with each.

Communion with the Father
The essence of the Father's communion with us is, Owen says, *love*. Perhaps there is a little deliberate provocation there, for Owen was acutely aware that we tend not to think of the Father as a lover, but instead shy away from him in our belief that he is stern and thunderous in his transcendental distance from us:

> At the best, many think there is no sweetness at all in him towards us, but what is purchased at the high price of the blood of Jesus. It is true, that alone is the way of communication; but the free fountain and spring of all is in the bosom of the Father.[5]

---

4. John Owen, *The Works of John Owen*, ed. William H. Goold, 24 vols. (Johnstone & Hunter, 1850–55; republished Edinburgh: Banner of Truth, 1965–91), vol. 1, p. 112. All quotations here are from this, most accessible, edition. I have, however, removed all instances of italics found in this edition, not only since it is very unclear which are original, but also because they tend to be confusingly haphazard.

5. *Works of John Owen*, vol. 2, p. 32.

Owen observes what Jesus says in John 16:26–27, 'I am not saying that I will ask the Father on your behalf. No, *the Father himself* loves you . . .' (my emphasis). In fact, the Father is the very origin and fountain of love: 'Jesus Christ, in respect of the love of the Father, is but the beam, the stream; wherein though actually all our light, our refreshment lies, yet by him we are led to the fountain, the sun of eternal love itself.'[6] All the Father's love is given to us only in Christ (he compares the grace of God in the Spirit to the oil poured out on Aaron the High Priest's head: it is all poured on the head, just as all the Father's love is poured on Christ, but then it runs down onto his body, the church). The source of love, however, is the Father. 'Sit down a little at the fountain, and you will quickly have a farther discovery of the sweetness of the streams. You who have run from him, will not be able, after a while, to keep at a distance for a moment.'[7]

Communion with the Son
The next (and by far the longest) section of the work is dedicated to the Son's communion with us, the essence of which is *grace*. Here Owen suffuses the pages with the language and imagery of Song of Songs. Understanding it to be a parable of the love between Christ and his bride, the church, he keeps returning to it so as to make readers feel the sweetness of communion with the Son.

Owen starts by looking at some of 'the personal excellencies of the Lord Christ', for it is by appreciating them that 'the hearts of his saints are indeed endeared unto him'.[8] Christ is shown to the reader to be so irresistibly attractive ('a fit object for your choicest affections'[9]) that our hearts are allured. More, he is not only beautiful and desirable in himself; he delights in his beloved believers and gives himself over entirely to love for them. Thus he causes them to delight in him and give themselves over in love for him.

In all this, the Son is actually revealing the Father. It is no

---

6. Ibid. p. 23.
7. Ibid. p. 36.
8. Ibid. p. 59.
9. Ibid. p. 53.

wonder that what he reveals is utterly surprising, for without the Son, we would have no knowledge of the Father; we would be helplessly mired in idolatry, worshipping a god that was not at all the true and living God. The Son, then, is the revealer and mediator, through whom we have communion with the Father.

Next Owen moves on to look at what the Son has done for us. And what undergirds his argument here (and so much of his theology elsewhere) is his 'covenant theology'. Essentially, what Owen envisages is this: Adam was created to exist in a 'covenant of works' with God. That meant that only if Adam obeyed God would he live. Of course, he disobeyed. God, however, continued to relate to humanity by this covenant of works: if humans obeyed, they would live. None did. But in eternity the Father had entered into another covenant with the Son (the 'covenant of redemption') to save the elect; as a result, Christ came and fulfilled the covenant of works by obeying God. With a relationship with God thus earned, in Christ the elect are as righteous as Adam would have been had he obeyed, and are able to relate to God by way of a 'covenant of grace'.

How Christ is a mediator between God and us is thus dealt with through the specific lenses of this covenant theology (something vital for Owen); but Owen's basic point is just that, that Christ, in his life, death, resurrection and ascension is a mediator 'to bring us to an enjoyment of God'.[10]

Communion with the Spirit
Lastly, the Spirit's communion with us, the essence of which is *comfort*. The Spirit, he argues, is essentially a Spirit of sanctification. That means that, first, he sets people apart by giving them new birth; and secondly, he comforts those who have been set apart. By 'comfort' Owen is referring to the comfort of Christ, which is the only comfort the Spirit brings. That is, the Spirit makes communion with the Son and the Father both real and delightful, spreading their love and confirming the truth in our hearts. Where Satan comes to rob confidence and comfort, the Spirit brings assurance

---

10. Ibid. p. 78.

and enjoyment of the truth. And only the Spirit can do that: when on earth, Owen notes, Christ seemed to affect the hearts of his disciples so little, but when the Spirit came, their hearts were all aflame for him. 'And this is his work to the end of the world, – to bring the promises of Christ to our minds and hearts, to give us the comfort of them, the joy and sweetness of them.'[11]

All that said, Owen is aware that readers could view the Spirit as a mere impersonal force of God. Yet he is emphatic that, while the Spirit is sent out of the Father's love to communicate the Son's grace, still he comes of his own will. He is a real person, and as such can and must be related to: 'the Holy Ghost, being God, is no less to be invocated, prayed to, and called on, than the Father and Son'.[12] Thus, though he will never leave the elect, he will not in fact always console them, if, for example, they grieve or resist him (not, of course, that Owen believes the Spirit truly can be grieved 'or affected with sorrow; which infers alteration, disappointment, weakness, – all incompatible with his infinite perfections').[13]

Owen was clearly concerned that the Spirit was being ignored by many (especially by the rationalists of the day). But he saw the consequences as terrible: first, if the Spirit does not really enter believers, then believers have no real union with Christ and so no real consolation; secondly, if people do not really have the Spirit, then they must have a spirit of bondage instead, 'casting them into an un-son-like frame of spirit'.[14]

To conclude:

> The emanation of divine love to us begins with the Father, is carried on by the Son, and then communicated by the Spirit; the Father designing, the Son purchasing, the Spirit effectually working: which is their order. Our participation is first by the work of the Spirit, to an actual interest in the blood of the Son; whence we have acceptation with the Father.[15]

---

11. Ibid. p. 237.
12. Ibid. pp. 229–230.
13. Ibid. p. 265.
14. Ibid. p. 258.
15. Ibid. p. 180.

It is a powerful case Owen has built for being trinitarian. In unitarian worship one could never validly entertain such warm, close thoughts of the Father, never have real union with the Son or adoption by the Father. In other words, the Spirit would have no comfort or assurance to give us.

The Doctrine of Justification by Faith
Something Owen had affirmed in *Communion with God* was that, in order to fulfil the covenant of works, Christ had lived a life of active righteousness. Thus when believers are justified, it is not merely that their sins are dealt with by him on the cross; that active righteousness of his is also credited to them. Affirming that sparked off a debate: was the active righteousness of Christ credited to believers? Some felt that this undercut all motivation for believers themselves to live lives of active righteousness.

Twenty years after publishing *Communion with God*, Owen responded to his critics with *The Doctrine of Justification by Faith*. It was more than a response, though; it was a massive exegetical, doctrinal and historical argument for the fact that, since Christ is one person, he has one righteousness, and since believers are part of the body of Christ, that righteousness is theirs.

For all the skill of the argument, it is a difficult and badly arranged work. And yet it has been significant: William Grimshaw, the great eighteenth-century preacher, was converted upon reading it and being confronted with Owen's question 'whether he will trust unto his own personal inherent righteousness, or, in a full renunciation of it, betake himself unto the grace of God and the righteousness of Christ alone'.[16]

Christologia
After *Communion with God*, *Christologia* was a book Owen always had to write, Christology being one of his two governing 'heads' of doctrine (and Owen being so generally Christ-centred). Its main point was to argue (against Socinianism, a heresy that, among other things, denied the deity of Christ) that true faith

16. Ibid. p. 230.

is faith in the person of Christ. But Owen wanted to do more than argue that point: he wanted actually to build that faith in his readers. Such true faith, he believed, could only come about when someone came to apprehend and appreciate the love of Christ; thus 'the great end of the description given of the person of Christ, is that we may love him, and thereby be transformed into his image'.[17] In *Christologia*, then, Owen set out to fix his readers' eyes on Christ, to roll the truths about Christ around in their minds so that their affections begin to be warmed towards him. And it was, quite specifically, his readers' affections that he was reaching for through their minds: 'Affections are in the soul as the helm in the ship; if it be laid hold on by a skilful hand, he turneth the whole vessel which way he pleaseth.'[18]

Owen starts out by affirming that he will be Christ-centred and nothing else, for it is Christ (not Peter) who is the rock and promised cornerstone on which the church is built; it is he who, from eternity, was chosen by the Father to be head over all and Saviour of the elect. Indeed, Owen argues, we must be Christ-centred, for naturally 'we can have no direct intuitive notions or apprehensions of the divine'; only in Christ, the image of God, is God's inmost being shown to us.[19] Hence 'faith in Christ is the only means of the true knowledge of God'.[20]

Owen is quite unrelenting on the point. It is entirely possible, he says, to have the Scriptures themselves and still have no true knowledge of God, as the Jews prove. Faith in Christ, then, is foundational; when it is uprooted, the truth of every doctrine collapses. One can almost see Owen's head shaking for those who have only a 'notional knowledge' of the Scriptures.

Owen goes on to pile up proofs that it is only through Christ that God confers any benefit to us. What is unclear is whether he means that God blesses us only through the person of the *eternal* Son, or whether he means, more specifically, that God blesses us

17. Ibid. vol. 1, p. 27.

18. Ibid. vol. 7, p. 397.

19. Ibid. vol. 1, p. 65.

20. Ibid. p. 77.

only through the *incarnate* Son. On the one hand, he is clear that, even before the incarnation, the Father would send the Son to do his work (he quotes e.g. Zech. 2:8–9, where 'the LORD Almighty' says 'the LORD Almighty has sent me'). Later in the work and elsewhere he writes of 'Appearances of the Son of God under the old testament'.[21] But on the other hand, he compares God's being to the sun: if it

> itself should come down unto the earth, nothing could bear its heat and
> lustre . . . So is it with this eternal beam or brightness of the Father's
> glory. We cannot bear the immediate approach of the Divine Being; but
> through him, *as incarnate*, are all things communicated unto us, in a way
> suited unto our reception and comprehension.[22]

Quite apart from the question of why the humanity of Mary and Christ were not incinerated by the immediate approach of the Divine Being in the moment of conception, there seems to be a contradiction here. But that aside, his point is clear: God's blessings are to be found only in Christ.

In fact, Owen is so strong in his affirmation that God blesses only through Christ that he is forced to deal with the question of the Old Testament: Did God bless people without Christ then? Quite simply, no:

> the faith of the saints under the Old Testament did principally respect
> the person of Christ – both what it was, and what it was to be in the
> fullness of time, when he was to become the seed of the woman . . .
> this has been the foundation of all acceptable religion in the world since
> the entrance of sin. There are some who deny that faith in Christ was
> required from the beginning, or was necessary unto the worship of God,
> or the justification and salvation of them that did obey him. For, whereas
> it must be granted that 'without faith it is impossible to please God,'
> which the apostle proves by instances from the foundation of the world,
> Heb. xi. – they suppose it is faith in God under the general notion of it,

---

21. Ibid. vol. 17. pp. 215–233.
22. Ibid. vol. 1, p. 16; my emphasis.

without any respect unto Christ, that is intended. It is not my design to
contend with any, nor expressly to confute such ungrateful opinions –
such pernicious errors. Such this is, which – being pursued in its proper
tendency – strikes at the very foundation of Christian religion; for it
at once deprives us of all contribution of light and truth from the Old
Testament.[23]

What Owen is fighting in all this is the practice of those 'who
profess a respect unto the Divine Being and the worship thereof,
[but] seem to have little regard unto the person of the Son in
all their religion'.[24] Often that disregard for the Son is extremely
subtle:

> Of all that poison which at this day is diffused in the minds of men,
> corrupting them from the mystery of the Gospel, there is no part that
> is more pernicious than this one perverse imagination, that to believe
> in Christ is nothing at all but to believe the doctrine of the gospel.[25]

In other words, he feared for those who worship 'God' ('under the
general notion') and believe 'the gospel' but do not trust Christ.

After all this, we might wonder if Owen's Christ-centredness
has become overwrought. Has the person of Christ effectively
eclipsed or swallowed up the Father and the Spirit? Owen answers
that the very reason we are called so to love Christ is because the
Father loves him. 'And all love in the creation was introduced
from this fountain, to give a shadow and resemblance of it.'[26] That
is, our creaturely love for the Son is meant to be a reflection of that
first love of the Father's. Thus to be lovingly devoted to the Son is
not to disregard the Father. Far from it: 'therein consists the principal part of our renovation into his image. Nothing renders us so
like unto God as our love unto Jesus Christ.'[27] Loving the Son we

23. Ibid. pp. 101, 120.
24. Ibid. p. 107.
25. Ibid. p. 127.
26. Ibid. p. 144.
27. Ibid. p. 146.

become like the Father. Also, trusting the Son we become like the Son, for we always become like what we trust. So, when we trust Christ, we become like what the Father loves. We are conformed into the image of God.

Christologia ends with a glance into the future. Having looked at Christ from eternity past as the beloved of the Father, the chosen Saviour, Owen now turns to examine the man Jesus' entry into heaven in the ascension, which 'is a principal article of the faith of the church, – the great foundation of its hope and consolation in this world'.[28] The man's presence before the Father is our consolation, for there he intercedes for us; but he is also our hope, for there his resurrected body is the head and beginning of the new creation. From the past to the future, then, Christ is the proper beloved of both God and man.

The overall effect of reading Owen's Christology can be summed up simply: it is like reading an invitation:

> Do any of us find decays in grace prevailing in us; – deadness, coldness, lukewarmness, a kind of spiritual stupidity and senselessness coming upon us? Do we find an unreadiness unto the exercise of grace in its proper season, and the vigorous acting of it in duties of communion with God, and would we have our souls recovered from these dangerous diseases? Let us assure ourselves there is no better way for our healing and deliverance, yea, no other way but this alone, – namely, the obtaining a fresh view of the glory of Christ by faith, and a steady abiding therein. Constant contemplation of Christ and his glory, putting forth its transforming power unto the revival of all grace, is the only relief in this case.[29]

Pneumatologia

While Owen believed that pneumatology was the second governing 'head' of doctrine, he was keenly aware that the person and work of the Spirit had always been badly neglected. In fact, he wrote, 'I know not any who ever went before me in this design of

---

28. Ibid. p. 235.
29. Ibid. p. 395.

representing the whole economy of the Holy Spirit.'[30] But such was the ambitious aim of *Pneumatologia*, to lay out a complete theology of the Spirit and his work.

In part, Owen was stung into writing by some views of the Spirit that he believed were threatening the health of the church. In the Roman Catholic Church, the Spirit had been replaced by the sacramental system; among the Quakers, the Spirit was being treated almost as a different God, delivering experiences and revelations entirely unconnected to Christ and the Scriptures; the Socinians thought of the Spirit as an impersonal force; and in far too many other places, the Spirit was simply forgotten or ignored.

After explaining the necessity of the task, Owen starts by looking at who the Spirit is. He is the spirit or breath of the Father and the Son, which means that, just

> as the vital breath of a man hath a continual emanation from him, and yet is never separated utterly from his person or forsaketh him, so doth the Spirit of the Father and the Son proceed from them by a continual divine emanation, still abiding one with them.[31]

However, while that speaks of the deity of the Spirit, it does not establish the fact of his 'distinct personality'. And it is this that he needed to prove against the Socinians. So Owen goes to Matthew 28:19, where God is named as Father, Son and Holy Spirit:

> Now, no man will or doth deny but that the Father and the Son are distinct persons. Some, indeed, there are who deny the Son to be God; but none are so mad as to deny him to be a person . . . Now, what confusion must this needs introduce, to add to them, and to join equally with them, as to all the concerns of our faith and obedience, the Holy Ghost, if he be not a divine person even as they![32]

---

30. Ibid. vol. 3, p. 7.

31. Ibid. p. 55.

32. Ibid. p. 72.

Moreover, the Spirit is said to have personal qualities: he understands, chooses, acts, teaches, he can be tested, grieved, blasphemed and lied to.

From there Owen goes on to look at the *work* of the Spirit, first of all in creation. The Spirit, he sees, essentially has a quickening, life-giving role in creation. That is, as a dove broods over her eggs, so the Spirit nourishes and imparts vital power into creation. In fact, this is his ongoing role, and not just what he did in the original act of creation: every year, after winter, it is the Spirit who causes everything to come to fresh life (Ps. 104:29–30). And so, in creation, the Spirit testifies to his proper work, which is the work of new creation.

Owen then shows the Spirit at work in the Old Testament, inspiring prophecy and the writing of Scripture, working miracles and enabling people (Samson to be strong, for example, and Bezalel to be a skilful craftsman). Indeed, 'we find everything that is good, even under the Old Testament, assigned unto him [the Spirit] as the sole immediate author of it'.[33] But, as in creation, his work there is preparatory for the work of new creation when, just as God once breathed (or 'spirated') life into Adam, so Jesus would breathe the Spirit onto his disciples.

On, then, to the Spirit's true work. This begins with his work on Christ's humanity, for he is the head of the new creation. The man Jesus, Owen shows, is the one so anointed with the Spirit that he does everything only as he is equipped and empowered by the Spirit. By the Spirit he is cast out into the desert, by the Spirit he himself then casts out demons, does miracles, offers himself as a sacrifice and so on.

Owen became uniquely strident in his eagerness to present Christ as the Spirit-anointed man. The eternal Son, he suggested, did not act directly in the man Jesus. 'The only singular immediate act of the person of the Son on the human nature was the assumption of it into subsistence with himself.'[34] After the Son had assumed human nature in Mary's womb it was the Spirit that

---

33. Ibid. p. 151.
34. Ibid. p. 160; cf. ibid. vol. 1, p. 225.

acted directly on the man. The man, then, did not have a divine
nature he could wheel out in times of need; he had to trust entirely
to the Spirit. Any other movements 'of the Son towards the human
nature were voluntary', so that, when for example on the cross
Jesus cried 'My God, my God, why have you forsaken me?', what
happened was that 'the human nature complained of its desertion
and dereliction by the divine', since at that point the divine nature
was no longer consoling the human.[35] It is an intriguing theory
that powerfully upholds the full humanity of Christ. One has to
wonder, though: can we really talk here of the one incarnate person
of Christ when God the Son only relates occasionally to the man
Jesus, and normally relates through another person (the Spirit)?

From the work of the Spirit on Christ, the head of the new creation, Owen proceeds to the work of the Spirit on Christ's body,
the church. By the Spirit, the Son gives *us* what the Father gave
him by the Spirit. The Spirit, then, is the one who unites us to God
so that, where we would merely have cowered before the Father
as our Judge and Creator, now by the Spirit, with the Son we cry,
'Abba!' 'As the descending of God towards us in love and grace
issues or ends in the work of the Spirit in us and on us, so all our
ascending towards him begins therein.'[36]

This work in us begins with regeneration. Without the Spirit,
we would be capable of altering ourselves superficially, though
we could never actually be renewed. But the Spirit brings true
and radical renewing, taking away our stony hearts and giving us
new ones. Thus he gives life and light, as he did back in the dark,
lifeless original creation. This work of regeneration had in fact
been done on all the elect under the Old Testament. 'The elect
of God were not regenerate one way, by one kind of operation
of the Holy Spirit, under the Old Testament, and those under
the New Testament [by] another.'[37] After all, none can ever enter
the kingdom without being born again of the Spirit. Yet regeneration is, by its very nature, a new creation work, and is therefore

---

35. Ibid. vol. 3, p. 161.
36. Ibid. p. 200.
37. Ibid. p. 214.

particularly associated with Christ's coming to usher in the new creation.

With some, Owen felt it necessary to argue for our need of regeneration; but with others, it was more a case of clarifying what regeneration looks like. Against certain 'enthusiasts' he argued, 'regeneration doth not consist in enthusiastical raptures, ecstasies, voices, or anything of the like kind'.[38] Why? Because the Spirit is the Spirit of the Creator, and so does not work against his creation, but with it, by means of the faculties of his creatures. 'He doth not come upon them with involuntary raptures, using their faculties and powers as the evil spirit wrests the bodies of them whom he possesseth.'[39] That said, Owen was no rationalist, and was quite aware that 'many of those who have been really made partakers of this gracious work of the Holy Spirit have been looked on in the world, which knows them not, as mad, enthusiastic, and fanatical'.[40]

To show that belief in regeneration is necessary, but not mad, novel nor needing to entail enthusiastic excesses, Owen then looks through Augustine's account of his own spiritual pilgrimage and regeneration in the *Confessions*. He recounts how Augustine was ruled by his appetites and desires, incapable of choosing any differently. Then, *through the Bible*, God changed his heart with all its desires; and with his affections now won to Christ he was able for the first time to choose freely for the good. The lesson is clear: there were no raptures or ecstasies, but without that change in his heart Augustine would have remained a slave to his old ways.

After that initial, instantaneous work of regeneration, the Spirit then works progressively to sanctify those who are part of the new creation. This sanctification, Owen is most careful to argue, is never something we can do for ourselves (that would be mere moralism); it is a work of the Spirit. And the Spirit does it by exciting and affecting us by the gospel, making us acquire a taste for the Lord and his ways. In fact, 'holiness is nothing but the implanting, writing and realizing of the gospel in our

---

38. Ibid. p. 224.
39. Ibid. p. 225.
40. Ibid. p. 226.

souls'.[41] Thus true holiness is all about relating to Christ; it is not about giving something back to God as if to fulfil our end of some bargain.

Because growth in holiness is about the 'realizing of the gospel in our souls', it must happen in the same way as our initial salvation. That is, just as we are justified by the blood of Christ, so we are sanctified by the blood of Christ. 'The Holy Ghost actually communicates the cleansing, purifying virtue of the blood of Christ unto our souls and consciences, whereby we are freed from shame, and have boldness towards God.'[42] By faith, then, our consciences are freed from guilt and we are able to grow in heart-felt love for God, which is the essence of holiness.

Sanctification is the Spirit's work of renewing a sin-scarred creation, and that means conforming us into the image of God, as we were created to be. That being the case, it cannot be 'any one faculty of the soul or affection of the mind or part of the body that is sanctified, but the whole soul and body, or the entire nature, of every believing person'.[43] Sanctification is a work of complete healing, making believers beautiful and whole, a work that will be perfected in our resurrection. Thus holiness, Owen stresses, is an eternal thing, the beginning of the indestructible new creation.

There is another aspect to Owen's theology of sanctification, and it is one that starts to take over as he continues his examination of the subject. As he goes on, Owen relies more and more on Aquinas's view that in sanctification the Spirit infuses habits into us. By this infusion, the old habits of sin are starved, and new habits are formed in us, inclining us to 'the duties of obedience'.

This use of Aquinas reveals some interesting ambivalences in Owen. Aquinas's talk of habits was drawn directly from Aristotle (and Owen actually quotes Aristotle here with approval, showing he is quite aware of his sources), yet Owen was clearly in two minds about him. On the one hand, he could happily and repeatedly turn to Aristotle in his theology; on the other, he could refer

---

41. Ibid. pp. 370–371.

42. Ibid. p. 445.

43. Ibid. p. 417.

to his influence as a 'contagion' that was rightly 'vomited out' by the first Reformers, only to creep back in to pollute the Reformed churches 'like Greeks out of the belly of the Trojan horse'.[44]

And the use of Aquinas in his discussion of sanctification produces similar tensions. Before he spoke of habits, Owen spoke of the Spirit transforming us *from the inside out*, winning our hearts and in that way changing our behaviour; but in Aquinas's thinking, we become holy *from the outside in* as we work at developing virtuous habits. And this is how Owen can now sound: 'Frequency of acts doth naturally increase and strengthen the habits whence they proceed . . . They grow and thrive in and by their exercise . . . The want thereof is the principal means of their decay.'[45] In places it sounds as if the habits themselves (church attendance etc.) almost have an innate ability to sanctify, and in such instances, Owen's talk of holiness as being essentially about a heart won for Christ is exchanged for something less obviously relational, where at times it begins to look as if holiness is, after all, something we give to God: 'Without the holiness prescribed in the gospel, we give nothing of that glory unto Jesus Christ which he indispensably requireth . . . He saves us freely by his grace; but he requires that we should express a sense of it.'[46]

Owen finishes the work with an argument for the necessity of holiness. Almost every conceivable motivation is set forth, from the being of God to our goal of conformity to the image of God. One, perhaps surprising, major motivation is our election in eternity:

> It is the eternal and immutable purpose of God, that all who are his in a peculiar manner, all whom he designs to bring unto blessedness in the everlasting enjoyment of himself, shall antecedently thereunto be made holy. This purpose of his God hath declared unto us, that we may take no wrong measures of our estate and condition, nor build hopes or expectations of future glory on sandy foundations that will fail us.[47]

---

44. *Biblical Theology*, pp. 678, 680.
45. *Works of John Owen*, vol. 3, p. 389.
46. Ibid. p. 650.
47. Ibid. p. 591.

In other words, God *will* make the elect holy, and thus I must be sure that I am holy if ever I am to be sure that I am one of the elect. Christ, Owen held, died only for the elect, and so my assurance of salvation cannot be found in the cross if I am not one of the elect. 'Neither have we any ground to suppose that we are built on that foundation of God which standeth sure, unless we depart from all iniquity.'[48] This was commonly employed Puritan logic, and yet how it should be used was relatively controversial. Many Puritans wrestled with the extent to which it is right to rest our assurance of salvation on our works, and whether true holiness can be motivated thus.

Appendices

In the years that followed the publication of *Pneumatologia*, Owen produced a number of appendices for the work.[49] *The Reason of Faith* set out how, without having to rely on any pope, we can believe Scripture to be the Word of God. Owen believed that many Protestant writers were being overly rationalistic in how they dealt with the question, making faith in Scripture dependent on complex external arguments. While those arguments may be right, he argued, 'We believe the Scripture to be the word of God with divine faith for its own sake only; or, our faith is resolved into the authority and truth of God only as revealing himself unto us therein and thereby.'[50]

The Causes, Ways and Means of Understanding the Mind of God defended the Protestant view that all Christians have a right to interpret the Bible for themselves, and do not need to rely on the pope and his official interpretation. Owen therefore looked at the vital role of the Spirit (and the means he uses) in enabling us to understand scriptures that otherwise would be dead letters to us.

---

48. Ibid. pp. 593–594.
49. The original treatise of *Pneumatologia* makes up vol. 3 of Owen's *Works*. These subsequent appendices make up vol. 4, but are presented there as part of *Pneumatologia*, since they were intended to be a continuation of the work.
50. *Works of John Owen*, vol. 4, p. 70.

JOHN OWEN 93

Having looked at how the Spirit enables us to read and trust Scripture, Owen then turned to examine *The Work of the Holy Spirit in Prayer*. Finally, a double-barrelled work completed the appendices: *The Holy Spirit as Comforter* dealt with much the same material as covered in *Communion with God*; and *Spiritual Gifts* looked at how the Spirit grants gifts for the building up of the church.

Hebrews

It would be rude to leave Owen without mentioning his massive, seven-volume commentary on Hebrews. The trouble is, commenting on commentaries can get very tedious, which is why I have avoided doing so in these introductions. But we can note the revealing significance of the work for Owen without bursting the bounds of this book.

It is not just that the commentary reveals Owen to be a first-rate linguist and exegete, capable of weaving together close textual analysis and doctrinal discussion; it is that Hebrews functioned in many ways as a complete theology for him. First, he believed it is a proclamation of Christ; but it is a message about him told through a comprehensive biblical theology that outlines the entire story and purpose of the Old Testament (especially the law), even managing to outline the history of the world from creation through to the millennium and final rest. It is yet more testimony to how Owen saw all things centred on Christ.

Going on with Owen

Owen, it has to be said, was pretty merciless towards his readers. He expected them to be serious and committed. He once wrote in a preface, 'Reader . . . If thou art, as many in this pretending age, a sign or title gazer, and comest into books as Cato into the theatre, to go out again – thou hast had thy entertainment; farewell!'[51] There are no gentle introductions, there is often little sense to the order of a book, and, bluntly, he does go on a bit. But

---

51. Ibid. vol. 10, p. 149.

all that is nothing to the way he writes. It feels as if Latin was his
real native tongue, and so, when he tries to write in English, the
result is uncomfortably constipated. Thus, trying to imbibe Owen
in large doses can be a bit like drinking rather too much Horlicks.
J. I. Packer's suggested medicine is to read Owen out loud, which
can help a bit. But, to be honest, whether read, said, chanted or
rapped, Owen is tough meat.

For all that, there is simply no substitute for going straight to
the horse's mouth. Probably the easiest and most rewarding place
to start is *Communion with God*. For a nicely accessible, modernized
version, I recommend Kelly M. Kapic and Justin Taylor (eds.),
Communion with the Triune God (Wheaton: Crossway, 2007), but it
is also available in vol. 2 of *The Works of John Owen*, ed. William
H. Goold, 24 vols. (Johnstone & Hunter, 1850–55; republished
Edinburgh: Banner of Truth, 1965–91). After that, *Christologia*
(*Works*, vol. 1) is well worth a read. *Pneumatologia* (*Works*, vol. 3) is
best left to the more keen. These texts are all freely available on
www.ccel.org, but really all Owen's works are too lengthy to be
read on a computer screen. Last, the commentary on Hebrews:
the seven volumes are obviously off-putting, but just a look at the
short preceding articles in the first Hebrews volume (*Works*, vol.
17) is worth it.

After that, probably the best introduction to Owen's life is Peter
Toon's now-classic biography *God's Statesman: The Life and Work of
John Owen: Pastor, Educator, Theologian* (Exeter: Paternoster, 1971).
As for his thought, try Sinclair Ferguson, *John Owen on the Christian
Life* (Edinburgh: Banner of Truth, 1987).

John Owen timeline

1616	Owen born; William Shakespeare dies
1628	Enters Queen's College, Oxford; John Bunyan born
1637	Leaves Oxford for a private chaplaincy
1642	Civil war begins; moves to London and experiences assurance of salvation
1643	Becomes minister at Fordham; marries Mary Rooke
1646	Moves to Coggeshall and becomes a Congregationalist
1649	Charles I executed; Owen preaches to Parliament; to Ireland as Cromwell's chaplain
1651	Appointed Dean of Christ Church, Oxford
1652	Appointed Vice-Chancellor of Oxford University
1657	Steps down as Vice-Chancellor; *Communion with God* published
1660	Charles II crowned; Bunyan imprisoned as Puritanism begins to be repressed
1663–4	Begins to live and pastor in and around London
1668–84	Commentary on Hebrews published
1674	*Pneumatologia* published
1675	First wife, Mary, dies
1676	Marries Dorothy D'Oyley
1679	*Christologia* published; John Bunyan publishes *The Pilgrim's Progress*
1683	Owen dies in Ealing

4. AMERICA'S THEOLOGIAN

Jonathan Edwards

And if they had been taught aright,
Small children carried bedwards
Would shudder lest they meet that night
The God of Mr. Edwards.

Abraham's God, the Wrathful One,
Intolerant of error –
Not God the Father or the Son
But God the Holy Terror.
(Phyllis McGinley, 'The Theology of Jonathan Edwards')

For too long Jonathan Edwards suffered his reputation as the horrid old preacher of 'Sinners in the Hands of an Angry God'. As a two-dimensional caricature (little more than a starch collar and a snarl) he could be dismissed easily. But in recent decades Edwards has begun to be rediscovered as a theologian of the broadest concerns and the highest calibre, so that many now regard him as America's greatest.

Edwards's life

In fact, Jonathan Edwards was self-consciously British. Born in East Windsor, Connecticut, in 1703, more than seventy years before the American Revolution, he lived and died as an aristocratic member of a colony he thought was as English as Kent. Like Kent, New England felt uncomfortably close to the Catholic influence of France (the colony of New France was not far away to the north and west); the difference to Kent was that East Windsor was in frontier territory, prone to Indian attack.

Jonathan's father, the Reverend Timothy Edwards, was a minister in the New England Puritan tradition (though we should not let the family's respectability fool us: Jonathan's 'grandmother was an incorrigible profligate, his great-aunt committed infanticide, and his great-uncle was an ax-murderer'[1]). Timothy Edwards was also a revival preacher, and this would prove key in the formation of Jonathan's mind. His preaching led to a short-lived spiritual 'awakening' in Jonathan when he was nine, making him intensely religious for a season. The fact that the phase soon passed would make him, as an adult, suspicious of religious enthusiasm as any sure guide to spiritual health.

Aged thirteen, he went to study at what was to become Yale University. That meant entering a rowdy world of rum, guns and riotous adolescent antics that was never Jonathan's scene. Bookish, hard-working and serious, he was not given to easy social banter and lounging, and so struggled to fit in. Coupled with that, a near-fatal illness triggered a period of spiritual turmoil that made him difficult company. Then, one day, reading 1 Timothy 1:17, 'a sense of the glory of the divine being' struck him in a way it never had before.[2] And this time it was no passing sense: over the months that followed he would wander alone through woods and fields (a lifelong habit), marvelling at the glory of Christ revealed

---

1. George M. Marsden, *Jonathan Edwards: A Life* (New Haven: Yale University Press, 2003), p. 22.

2. *Works of Jonathan Edwards*, 26 vols. (New Haven: Yale University Press, 1957–2008), vol. 16, p. 792.

there, or he would open his Bible to enjoy the beauty of Christ laid
before him.

In the summer of 1722, aged eighteen, he went to assist the
pastor of a small church in New York City. It was there that he
began his habit of jotting down his thoughts in notebooks, and it
was there that he compiled a list of seventy 'Resolutions', binding
himself to live in specific, holy disciplines. For example, Resolution
4: 'Resolved, never to do any manner of Thing, whether in Soul or
Body, less or more, but what tends to the glory of God; nor be,
nor suffer it, if I can avoid it.'[3] He committed himself to reading
them once a week, keeping a close eye on how well he scored each
time. The result, his journal reveals, was that he was a yo-yo of
spiritual highs and lows. He was spiritually alive at last, but struggling, relying too much on his own strength.

The next year his father engineered a pastorate for him in
Bolton, back near East Windsor. It was a position he was uncomfortably shoehorned into, and so when Yale offered him a position
as a tutor, he quickly left Bolton. The post was not Yale's only
attraction, though: the thirteen-year-old Sarah Pierpont was also
there. Within two years they were engaged, two more and they
were married.[4] It was the beginning of what Jonathan would
call an 'uncommon union' of affection (a union that was to bear
eight sons and three daughters, all but one daughter living to
adulthood). Through his love for the more approachable Sarah it
becomes clear that while Jonathan was reserved in public, personally he was warm and affectionate. And that is important to notice:
warm affections were crucial for Edwards.

At around the same time that Jonathan was getting married,
his grandfather, the formidable Solomon Stoddard, had him
appointed as his assistant pastor in Northampton, back up the
Connecticut valley. Within two years, Stoddard had died and
Edwards had succeeded him. However, Stoddard had been the
pastor of Northampton for nearly sixty years, and had in that time

3. Ibid. p. 753.
4. Sarah was a young sweetheart and fiancée indeed, but this was not
    considered inappropriate at the time.

accrued an almost papal authority. Edwards would never escape his shadow. And that meant having to live with certain practices he disapproved of, such as giving communion to those who showed no sign of being converted (Stoddard had held that communion was able to convert them).

For five years Edwards pastored this sizable church of some thirteen hundred. Then, in 1734, he preached the funeral sermon for a young man who had died suddenly. It jerked many from their spiritual complacency and brought them, Edwards believed, to true conversion. A spirit of renewal began to sweep the town: people met to pray and sing hymns, and crowds came to his home for counsel. And with the conversion of a notorious 'company-keeper', the flames of revival intensified and spread to other towns. Edwards saw hundreds being converted, and extraordinarily, illness became unknown in the town.

All the while, Edwards was fuelling the revival with the message 'Despair, but for Christ!' Some, though, seemed only to hear 'Despair!' and after just over a year of awakening, Edwards's uncle committed suicide by slitting his throat. At that, things seemed to unravel. For months the town had seemed free of physical and mental illness, but at this, scores now seemed suddenly tempted to follow suit, hearing voices that urged them to commit suicide. Thus the revival left a curious legacy: on the one hand, Edwards recorded the events in *A Faithful Narrative of the Surprising Work of God*, a work that became the inspiration for revivals that soon began on both sides of the Atlantic; on the other hand, with the revival in Northampton over and lives returned to much the same as before, Edwards was left to reflect on how he had assumed genuine conversion too quickly in those touched by the awakening.

It was not as if Edwards gave up on the very idea of revival. Far from it: he prayed for it incessantly. Then George Whitefield, perhaps the main revival preacher in England, came to the colony, and in 1740 arrived in Northampton. With him came a new awakening, greater than the first. It would provide the background for the most notorious event of Edwards's life. The following July, with revival still coursing through the region, Edwards visited nearby Enfield, and preached the sermon 'Sinners in the Hands

of an Angry God'. In contrast to George Whitefield, there were
never any flashy theatrics to Edwards's preaching; it was his quiet
intensity that seemed to make him so compelling. But before this
sermon was done, 'there was a great moaning and crying throughout the whole house. What shall I do to be saved. Oh I am going
to Hell. Oh what shall I do for Christ.'[5] Edwards asked for silence,
but the shrieks and wails now drowned him out and he was forced
to head down into the congregation to minister to individuals.

What the sermon *does not* show is *what* Edwards always sought
to preach. Hell, after all, was just one truth Edwards believed in,
and it would be extremely naive (and just plain wrong) to take the
sermon on its own as representative of Edwards's overall thought.
What the sermon *does* show is *how* Edwards always sought to
preach. His aim was to preach every doctrine thoroughly and in
such a way that his hearers felt the reality of the truths in question.
What they were brought to feel in this case was the fearful danger
of being a sinner in an unrepentant state; but in another sermon
they would be brought to feel 'The Pleasantness of Religion' or the
'Safety, Fullness and Sweet Refreshment in Christ'.

After two years, this second revival also died down, and, as after
the first, the people's old ungodly patterns of behaviour began
to resurface. Only now, the people were no longer prepared to
put up with being rebuked for their ways. Thus relations between
Edwards and his parishioners (relations that had never really been
warm) became progressively more strained. Then Edwards did the
unthinkable: he proposed abolishing 'Pope' Stoddard's old practice
of admitting the unconverted to communion. By this time Edwards
had served Northampton as pastor for just over twenty years, but
still the church was unable to countenance defiance of their old
patriarch. The council moved swiftly to remove Edwards from the
pastorate (though months of awkwardness remained as, for want
of any other preacher, they asked him to preach most weeks).

Early the next year (1751), he took up an invitation to be
the minister of Stockbridge, a mission station based among the

5. Stephen Williams, diary, 8 July 1741 (typescript), Storrs Memorial Library,
   Longmeadow, Massachusetts.

Mohican Indians. The evangelization of the Indians was a cause that had been growing in his mind for some time. Just a few years earlier, the missionary David Brainerd had stayed for four months with the Edwards family to recover from what turned out to be fatal tuberculosis. It shows what an impact Brainerd made that, almost as soon as he had died, Edwards began work on a biography, *The Life of David Brainerd*, which turned out to be one of the most influential accounts of mission ever. Other than fortifying Edwards's concern for the Indians, though, it is hard to know quite how much Brainerd actually influenced Edwards. It is easy, for example, to imagine the author of 'Sinners in the Hands of an Angry God' goggling at a comment Brainerd made of the Indians, 'It was surprizing [*sic*] to see how their hearts seemed to be pierced with the tender and melting invitations of the Gospel, when there was not a word of terror spoken to them.'[6] In fact, though, it seems that each found the other encouraging simply because of their sheer likeness of heart and mind. Certainly, Brainerd's striking comment is reflective of Edwards's own emphases.

Something that made Edwards's work with the Indians different from his previous ministry was the fact that the Bible had not been translated into their language. Edwards thus sought to teach them English. Interestingly, he was also eager to teach them to sing, for music, he believed 'has a powerful efficacy to soften the heart into tenderness, to harmonize the affections, and to give the mind a relish for objects of a superior character'.[7]

They were difficult years in Stockbridge: the English settlers were constantly feuding, and the tension was not helped by the perpetual threat of attack. The smallness and remoteness of the place did, however, give Edwards more time than he had ever had before. This he invested in writing. In particular, he wanted to write in defence of Calvinism.

The key work here was *The Freedom of the Will*, and Edwards saw it as foundational since (like Luther and Calvin before him) he believed the idea that we are self-determining (that we can

---

6. *Works of Jonathan Edwards*, vol. 7, p. 307.

7. Ibid. vol. 16, p. 411.

determine our own choices) cuts right against the gospel. Of course, he saw, I choose to do what I want to do, and in that sense my will is free. With complete freedom I choose to drink this cup of tea. But what I want is shaped entirely by what I love. I choose to drink tea and not sewage because I like tea and am less partial to sewage. Just so, we cannot ever choose God, for we do not naturally love him, and we only choose what we love. Thus, unless a divine and supernatural light breaks in to reorient our hearts to love God, we cannot choose to do so.

The other main apologia for Calvinism was *Original Sin*, a defence of the idea that our destinies are determined by another, since we inherit both guilt and corruption from Adam. But in his articulation of this old doctrine, Edwards made a unique move. So strong was he in his bid to annihilate any self-determination in the creature that he came up with the following: 'God's uphold-ing created substance, or causing its existence in each successive moment, is altogether equivalent to an *immediate production out of nothing*, at each moment.'[8] Now, making God recreate all things out of nothing each new moment certainly stops the creature from having any self-determination, but at what cost? God is now (and at each moment) the creator of a fallen world.

While Edwards was completing *Original Sin*, revival broke out at the College of New Jersey in Princeton. And when they began looking for a new president, Edwards seemed the obvious candi-date. Edwards, though, was reluctant. He had begun preparations for two 'great works' he was eager to complete, *A History of the Work of Redemption*, and *The Harmony of the Old and New Testaments*. They would be his final masterpieces, the encapsulation of his life's thought. At Princeton they were quite understanding, though, and so in January 1758 Edwards took up the post of president there.

A month later, Edwards had himself inoculated against the smallpox that was raging through New Jersey. The procedure went awry, though, and Edwards ended up contracting the disease in his

---

8. Ibid. vol. 3, p. 402, italics original. Edwards seemed to view each creative moment rather like a still on a film reel being played on the screen of God's mind. Played all together, the stills then give the effect of time and movement.

mouth and throat. It became impossible for him to swallow, and on March 22 he finally succumbed.

Edwards's thought

In order to grasp the overall shape and feel of Edwards's thought, we will look first at his *Religious Affections*, and then try to piece together the gist of his two projected 'great works', *A History of the Work of Redemption*, and *The Harmony of the Old and New Testaments*. Through them we will also get to sample a number of his other writings, such as *The End for Which God Created the World*.

Religious Affections

In 1746, shortly after the second (Whitefield-inspired) awakening in Northampton, Edwards published his *Religious Affections*. The aim was twofold: to show, against the critics of revival, that religious affections are necessary and important; and to show others, perhaps swept along by wonderful religious experiences, how such things could be misinterpreted. Again and again Edwards had been fooled into believing that a person was truly converted because of how they seemed, only to find them slipping back later into coldness towards Christ. So, while he realized that only God can know the heart for sure, he wanted to set out what are (and what are not) reliable indications that a person is truly converted.

What makes the *Religious Affections* such a striking read is not only the extraordinary penetration of Edwards's insights, but also the way he appeals to the reader. In all his preaching and writing, he always sought to have his audience feel the truths in question. It would therefore have been entirely incongruous, to his mind, to speak of religious affections in an unaffecting, lifeless way. The result is unforgettable.

Part 1: The nature and importance of the affections

In Edwards's society, most people would have had a theoretical knowledge of at least some Christian basics. But so do devils, thought Edwards. Mere knowledge of the gospel he thus saw as something entirely different from true conversion. Instead, he argued, 'True religion, in great part, consists in holy affections.'[9] By this he meant that the true convert is palpably moved beyond indifference ('the motion of the blood and animal spirits begins to be sensibly altered') to love for Christ and joy in him.[10]

A whole understanding of what it is to be a person was implied. Edwards argues that it is our affections that drive everything we do: we seek money because we love it; we run from danger because we love our lives; and so on. Thus when we receive the Spirit (who is eternally the love between the Father and the Son), his work is to bring us to share that love for the Father and the Son. Love, then (by which he meant a real engagement of the heart), is 'the first and chief of the affections, and the fountain of all the affections'.[11] It is when we are brought to love Christ that other, Christian affections follow: we begin to be filled with joy and gratitude; we begin to hate sin; and so on.

This, Edwards says, is why God has ordained preachers. It is not that we might hear mere 'expositions on the Scripture' that do not rouse the affections. Rather, preachers 'stir up the pure minds of the saints, and quicken their affections' by setting the things of the gospel before them 'in their proper colors . . . And particularly, to promote those two affections in them . . . love and joy.'[12] This preachers do especially by presenting the cross, for the 'glory and beauty of the blessed Jehovah . . . is there exhibited in the most affecting manner that can be conceived of',[13] though in fact all God's ways of redemption are so arranged

> as to have the greatest, possible tendency to reach our hearts in the most tender part, and move our affections most sensibly and strongly. How great cause have we therefore to be humbled to the dust, that we are no more affected![14]

9. Ibid. vol. 2, p. 95.

10. Ibid.

11. Ibid. p. 108.

12. Ibid. p. 116.

13. Ibid. p. 123.

14. Ibid. p. 124.

In contrast, sin is about hardness or coldness of heart. Such a heart, because it has no true love for Christ, cannot produce any good. Edwards was thus highly wary of those in his day who, sceptical of affections, taught that religion is essentially about the intellect choosing the logically correct path:

> They who condemn high affections in others, are certainly not likely to have high affections themselves . . . The right way, is not to reject all affections, nor to approve all; but to distinguish between affections, approving some, and rejecting others.[15]

Part 2: Unreliable signs of conversion

Through bitter experience, Edwards had learned to be extremely wary of the complexities and deceitfulness of the human heart, and the second part of the treatise is simply devastating in how completely it dismisses so many apparent indications of conversion as mere false signs. It is not that Edwards is saying that there is necessarily anything wrong with them; merely that they are unreliable guides to the real state of a heart.

Essentially, Edwards's point here is that, for all sorts of reasons, it is quite possible for a person to get whipped up into a spiritual 'high' that is entirely superficial. The crowd's cries of 'Hosanna!' can quickly turn to 'Crucify!' As such, the zeal and enthusiasm people show may come, not from any fundamental change in their hearts, but from the mere froth of passing emotion. In pointing this out, Edwards has made an important distinction: true religion, in great part, does consist in holy affections, but those affections are deep, though palpable, changes in the very grain of the heart and its inclinations; they are not to be confused with passions of the moment, which come and go with blood sugar levels.

Yet these passing (or false) enthusiasms can be extremely convincing: I can appear to be loving, I can seem to be under a strong conviction of my sin, be zealously involved in church activities, delight in hearing the Scriptures preached, love talking about

---

15. Ibid. p. 121.

religion and the Bible; through such things I can even convince myself and others that I am truly converted.

The overall effect of the section is distinctly unnerving, and the reader is left hungry for the next.

Part 3: True signs of conversion[16]

What marks out the affections of the truly born again is that they come from the Spirit. The Holy Spirit makes the heart of the believer holy. Holiness, Edwards explains, 'is as it were the beauty and sweetness of the divine nature', and this is what the Spirit imparts to the believer.[17] He communicates the goodness of his nature so that Christians, 'by reflecting the light of the Sun of Righteousness, do shine with the same sort of brightness, the same mild, sweet and pleasant beams'.[18] Edwards talks much of the 'sweetness' of Christ and how he makes Christians 'sweet'. But it would be a mistake to imagine Edwards slipping into sentimentality, for this 'sweetness' is no weak thing, but strength shown in the face of the natural slide into unpleasant viciousness.

In fact, Edwards sees that it is having a sense of the sweetness of God that is really what marks out the converted. He compares two men: one knows merely *that* honey is sweet; the other 'loves honey and is greatly delighted in it because he knows the sweet taste of it'.[19] So it is with conversion: it is not merely that I

---

16. Edwards lists twelve true signs of conversion, as he had listed twelve unreliable signs. However, boiling them down and presenting them one by one would border on cruelty to the reader! Instead I will simply try to present the gist of the section.

17. *Works of Jonathan Edwards*, vol. 2, p. 201.

18. Ibid. p. 347.

19. Ibid. p. 209. Stephen Holmes suggests that, since honey is more commonplace today, the illustration works less well than it would have done, and so provides his own illustration: 'I might have been told of a liquid that tastes of seaweed and peat smoke, and might even believe that this could be a pleasant experience, in the sense of giving intellectual consent to such a proposition, but only when I taste the whiskies of Islay will I really understand what is meant, and be seized by the desire

understand that God is sweet; it is that I now have a sense of and appreciation for that sweetness. I have tasted and seen.

This sense of the sweetness of divine things is essentially about enjoying the beauty of God. God, for Edwards, is distinguished from all other beings chiefly by his beauty, and it is beauty above all that stirs the affections and changes hearts. Thus true believers are impressed first by the beauty of God as he is in himself; they are not impressed primarily with what they gain from the gospel.

Seeing this enables Edwards to make some painfully piercing observations on Christian hypocrisy and hypocritical preaching of the gospel. The problems begin when the beauty of Christ is lost, for then the Christian message becomes nothing more than a cheap form of eternal fire insurance. But the hypocrite loves this, for the hypocrite most fundamentally loves himself and so is moved primarily by what God can do for him. That is, at root, the hypocrite does not love God, but himself, and simply likes the fact that he can be nicely served by God.

One way hypocrites can be unmasked is by the fact that, since their interest is essentially in themselves, they keep their eyes fixed not on 'the beauty of Christ, but the beauty of their experiences'; 'hypocrites, in their high affections, talk more of the discovery, than they do of the thing discovered'.[20] The worry is that, because of the self-love involved, such false affections tend actually to harden the heart in direct contrast to the true work of the Spirit, who makes believers always hungry to know and love God more, to hate sin more, and so on.

Hypocrites, because they have no true love for God, also misunderstand humility, thinking that it too is all about themselves. Instead of happily abandoning themselves for God, hypocrites

---

to discover more' (*God of Grace and God of Glory: An Account of the Theology of Jonathan Edwards* [Grand Rapids: Eerdmans, 2000], p. 162). Dare one quibble with such a fine illustration? Hardly, and yet to my knowledge there is one thing Islay whiskies lack that is important for Edwards's point: sweetness. But I stand prepared to be educated here.

20. *Works of Jonathan Edwards*, vol. 2, pp. 251, 252.

merely abandon certain things (e.g. wealth and pleasure), and do so only to fuel their own self-righteousness, selling 'one lust to feed another . . . a beastly lust to pamper a devilish one'.[21] And their lack of love for God becomes evident in the imbalance of their lives: claiming to love God but having no love for men, or loving people in church on Sunday but beating their wives on Monday.

Because true believers are affected by the Spirit, what moves them is nothing within themselves, but always the Spirit's revelation of the things of God in Scripture: 'Holy affections are not heat without light; but evermore arise from some information of the understanding, some spiritual instruction that the mind receives, some light or actual knowledge.'[22] It is by knowing God better that we love him more. Thus godly affections are not mere emotions, but are about having a taste or relish for the God revealed in Scripture. And this 'sense of the spiritual excellency and beauty of divine things, does also tend directly to convince the mind of the truth of the gospel' so that believers are no longer troubled by the truth of it, but bold to venture their all upon it.[23] The divine excellence of the gospel melts away prejudices against it. This is very different from those who place their faith fundamentally not on the gospel itself but on external attestations that the gospel is reliable. For them, the insufficiency of the evidence means that 'there will endless doubts and scruples remain'.[24]

Edwards ends the treatise by arguing that Christian practice is 'the chief of all the signs of grace', the best indication to others and to myself that I have been born again.[25]

> Christ is not in the heart of a saint, as in a sepulcher, or as a dead
> Saviour, that does nothing; but as in his temple, and as one that is alive
> from the dead. For in the heart where Christ savingly is, there he lives,

---

21. Ibid. p. 315.
22. Ibid. p. 266.
23. Ibid. p. 301.
24. Ibid. p. 304.
25. Ibid. p. 406.

and exerts himself after the power of that endless life, that he received at his resurrection.[26]

A History of the Work of Redemption

Before he died, Edwards was planning to write 'a great work, which I call *A History of the Work of Redemption*, a body of divinity in an entire new method, being thrown into the form of an history'.[27] It was to have started in eternity past, with a look at why God ever chose to create and redeem a world. It would then swoop down to tell the history of creation (heaven, earth and hell) from beginning to end. This, he believed, would be fittingly beautiful and entertaining, and thereby 'every divine doctrine, will appear to greatest advantage'. An ambitious plan indeed!

It might seem absurd to try to outline a work Edwards never wrote; however, he was clear that the first part would be based on his earlier work, *The End for Which God Created the World*, and the second part would be based on his earlier sermon series, *A History of the Work of Redemption*. So by getting to know those two earlier pieces we should get a good feel for what Edwards saw as the masterpiece that would encapsulate his theology.

The End for Which God Created the World

If *Religious Affections* reveals Edwards's pastoral insight, *The End for Which God Created the World* brilliantly displays the freshness of his mind and sheer creative panache. That said, it does not start well. A ten-page introduction is spent defining terms, the key ones being 'ultimate end' (something done for its own sake) and 'chief end' (the ultimate end most valued). But one can get along quite nicely without knowing exactly what Edwards is talking about here, and the section is best skimmed or skipped if you're feeling nervous.

Chapter 1: What reason tells us

Edwards does not believe that reason alone can establish what God's chief end or goal in creating the world was; that said, he

26. Ibid. p. 392.
27. Ibid. vol. 16, p. 727.

does think that what he is going to argue is rationally coherent, and that is what he sets out to show first. The reader needs to bear this in mind, for if the arguments of chapter 1 are read as logical proofs, they do look rather thin. For example, he will argue "'Tis a thing infinitely good in itself that God's glory should be known by a glorious society of created beings.'[28] In chapter 2 he will make a good, biblical case for this, but as it stands in chapter 1, the claim is not at all self-evident.

The argument begins by asserting that no rational account of God's goal in creation can suggest that God somehow needed creation. God, who existed before creation, cannot be dependent on creation. What, then, was his goal? It must have been what is most valuable; and that, of course, is himself. But what does that mean? Edwards looks at God's attributes or characteristics and says, 'If the world had not been created, these attributes never would have had any exercise.'[29] Certainly, this is unguarded language. Was the Father not good to the Son, for instance? At times in this section it can sound as if the God he is describing is a solitary being, not a Trinity of persons where, for example, the Son knows the Father: 'It seems to be a thing in itself fit and desirable, that the glorious perfections of God should be known, and the operations and expressions of them seen by other beings besides himself.'[30]

Then he comes to the nub of his argument: God's goal, he says, was 'to communicate of his own infinite fullness of good'.[31] God, he explains, is like a fountain of goodness, and delights to spread his own goodness and happiness, his knowledge of himself and joy in himself. None of this is to say that God is choosing to do any of this for his creatures as such. God had this delight before he had even chosen to create. Rather, God's great aim is to express

28. Ibid. vol. 8, p. 431.
29. Ibid. p. 429.
30. Ibid. pp. 430–431.
31. Ibid. p. 433. The implications of this are profound for understanding God's judgment and hell. Since communicating his goodness is God's ultimate aim, Edwards held that damnation is God's strange work, done not for its own sake but for the great end of the plan of redemption.

his goodness and happiness. But as soon as God decided to create, that aim meant that he would be all about communicating his goodness to his creatures. Thus 'God's acting for himself, or making himself his last end, and his acting for their sake, are not to be set in opposition'.[32]

With this, Edwards has brilliantly cut through a quandary. For if we say God's sole aim in creation is himself, we make God sound selfish, as if he is merely using us for his own purposes; but if we say God's sole aim is us and our good, we sound selfish, as if we were using God. But for Edwards, God's great goal *is* his own glory (God is not subservient to some higher purpose than himself); and yet that highest purpose is self-giving, not self-serving.

Edwards then turns to answer some potential objections. First, does this not actually make God dependent on creation, as if God needs creation in order that he might communicate his goodness? This is a position Edwards is determined to distance himself from. God, who is complete and happy in himself, is never about getting something from creation, but giving out of his natural, overflowing goodness. His pleasure 'is rather a pleasure in diffusing and communicating to the creature, than in receiving from the creature'.[33]

On the other hand, does this not all make God out to be a selfish cosmic egotist? Such a view Edwards had equally little tolerance for. He would rail against those who imagined a God who 'has no proper love or fervent affection but only a cool purpose and that he has no true delight or happiness in his Creatures'. For Edwards, God is no self-serving applause-seeker; his aim is to communicate and share his goodness and happiness, and that is generous, not selfish: 'in seeking himself, i.e. himself diffused and expressed (which he delights in, as he delights in his own beauty and fullness), he seeks their glory and happiness'.[34]

---

32. Ibid. p. 440.
33. Ibid. p. 448.
34. Ibid. p. 459.

Chapter 2: What Scripture tells us

Edwards begins the second chapter by machine-gunning his readers with Bible verses to prove that God is the Alpha and Omega, the origin and goal of all things, that all things are from him and for him, and that the end of all things is to glorify God. To glorify God, he shows, was always Christ's aim, as it is the point of the Christian life.

So Scripture shows the glory of God as the chief end of creation and redemption. But (and here is the key question) what, precisely, does Scripture mean by 'the glory of God'? Sometimes it is a phrase 'used to signify the second person in the Trinity'.[35] And this fits with the fact that, as well as working for his glory, God repeatedly says he is acting for the sake of his name, and 'the Name of the LORD' is another phrase used of Christ. Commenting elsewhere on Isaiah 30:27 ('See, the Name of the LORD comes from afar, / with burning anger and dense clouds of smoke; / his lips are full of wrath, / and his tongue is a consuming fire'), Edwards says, 'God's name is evidently spoken of as a person.'[36] Christ is the name and glory of God.

But still, what could that mean? In Scripture, he says, the glory of a thing is its weight, majesty and essence. But the word also 'often signifies a visible exhibition of glory; as in an effulgence or shining brightness, by an emanation of beams of light. Thus the brightness of the sun and moon and stars is called their "glory".'[37] And thus we see Christ described as the brightness of the Father's glory shining out (Heb. 1:3). As it turns out, Edwards seems to view light as the most essential and revealing synonym for glory. The image of light is closely associated with enlightenment and knowledge. But light also shines forth, and that image of glorious beams of light shining out captures Edwards's understanding of glory:

> What God has in view in neither of them, neither in his manifesting his
> glory to the understanding nor communication to the heart, is not that

35. Ibid. p. 512.
36. Ibid. vol. 21, p. 377.
37. Ibid. vol. 8, pp. 514–516.

he may receive, but that he [may] go forth: the main end of his shining forth is not that he may have his rays reflected back to himself, but that the rays may go forth.[38]

God's glory is his going out (in Christ) to make known and available his righteousness, wisdom, goodness and mercy. And this is why creation exists, so that his people might enjoy him. God's glory, then, is his grace (Edwards thinks the phrase 'according to the riches of his *glory*' in Ephesians 3:16 is equivalent to 'according to the riches of his *grace*' in Ephesians 1:7 [Authorized Version]). Thus Christ's death is the hour he is glorified, for it is then that he is revealed in his full graciousness, giving himself in love for his church. And thus the church is the glory of Christ, for it is the fruit of his self-giving grace.

Underneath the entire argument lie strong trinitarian foundations, which, although largely hidden, are worth being aware of. Some of Edwards's language (God's 'love for himself', for instance) can be quite misleading unless it is understood that Edwards is thinking of the Father's love for the Son. In fact, the whole shape of the work is trinitarian, especially in the second chapter. The reason God creates is to express and communicate to others the love that the Father has for the Son. And it is in that fellowship that we will enjoy a never-ending increase of happiness as 'the union will become more and more strict and perfect; nearer and more like to that between God the Father and the Son'.[39]

A History of the Work of Redemption *(sermon series)*[40]
It was only fitting that Edwards should move on to this subject next, for the history of redemption, in which God expresses and

---

38. Ibid. vol. 13, p. 496.
39. Ibid. vol. 8, p. 533. Edwards believed that both heaven and hell are progressive states, such that, as our love and union with God will ever develop in heaven, so hatred will ever worsen in hell.
40. This series of thirty sermons, preached in 1739, was put together as a book by others after Edwards's death (and appears as such in the two-volume Banner of Truth edition of his works); however, it should not

shares his love, *is* the end of creation. Edwards divides his history
into three parts that correspond to the Old Testament, the New
Testament and then subsequent church history up until Christ's
return.

Part 1: From creation to incarnation

In *The End for Which God Created the World* Edwards had already
begun his history with a look at God's intentions in eternity past.
Back then, the Father had appointed the Son to be the redeemer.
But then, as 'soon as ever man fell Christ entered on his medi-
atorial work'.[41] Immediately, the gospel was declared (in Gen. 3:15)
and God began to show mercy to sinners and save them through
Christ. Adam and Eve were even clothed with animal skins as
outward signs of the righteousness of Christ with which they were
now covered.

And redemption, Edwards is clear, was always through Christ:

> when we read in the sacred history [the Old Testament] what God did
> from time to time towards his church and people, and what he said to
> them, and how he revealed himself to them, we are to understand it
> especially of the second person of the Trinity. When we read after this of
> God's appearing time after time in some visible form or outward symbol
> of his presence, we are ordinarily if not universally to understand it of
> the second person of the Trinity.[42]

Judging by the time he gives to it in his writings, this was a point
that clearly concerned Edwards. He devoted entire papers (e.g.

Footnote 40 (*cont.*)
> be confused with the 'great work' that he intended, but never managed, to
> write. The sermon series was to provide the foundations for the second
> part of that work, but in his preparatory notes he makes it clear that he
> intended to expand his history to include significantly more on the history
> of the papacy and more on the history of heaven and hell, angels and
> demons, 'the state of departed saints' and the new creation.

41. *Works of Jonathan Edwards*, vol. 9, p. 129.
42. Ibid. p. 131.

'In what sense did the saints under the Old Testament believe in Christ to justification?') to arguing that it was 'plainly and fully revealed to the church of Israel' that Christ, the angel of the Lord, was a distinct person from the Father to be trusted, and in fact that the 'people of God trusted in this person to save them', knowing that he would come and make atonement for them.[43]

Then came the first revival, 'the first remarkable pouring out of the Spirit through Christ that ever was . . . in the days of Enos'.[44] This led to the salvation of men such as Enoch, who provided the first, important instance of a body being redeemed from death. It also set the pattern for the history to come: the work of redemption would be achieved mainly through great outpourings of the Spirit.

God also provided the church with prophecies and types (sacrifices as 'prototypes' of the cross etc.) to keep their hopes set on the coming redemption. But the 'greatest pledge and forerunner of the future redemption of Christ of any' was the exodus. It was not, though, as if the church was left with mere promises of the coming redemption. Christ himself was with them. It was he who wrought the exodus, appearing to Moses in the bush (which represented the human nature he would assume, being burned by the fire of God's wrath, but not consumed).

> Because this great mystery of the incarnation and suffering of Christ was here represented, therefore Moses says, I will turn aside and behold this great sight. A great sight he might well call it when there was to be seen represented God manifested in the flesh, and suffering a dreadful death, and rising from the dead.[45]

Then 'Christ went before 'em in a pillar of cloud and fire' and gave Moses the Ten Commandments with his own hand.[46]

More than the Ten Commandments, though, the whole law was a school of types so that 'the gospel was abundantly held forth to

---

43. Ibid. vol. 21, pp. 372, 389.
44. Ibid. vol. 9, p. 141.
45. Ibid. p. 175.
46. Ibid. p. 176.

that nation so that there is scarce any doctrine of it but is particularly taught and exhibited by some observance of this law'.[47] By this stage the reader should be clear that Edwards is very interested in types (something we will discuss more later). He believed that there are three sorts of types: *institutions*, of which the greatest were the sacrifices; *events*, of which the greatest was the exodus; and *individuals* who were themselves types, of whom the greatest was David (God's anointed who redeemed Jerusalem, the greatest type of the church).

David was also a prophet who sang of 'those great things of Christ's redemption that had been the hope and expectation of God's church and people from the very beginning'.[48] And as the time of Christ's coming approached, such prophesying increased, for God set up permanent schools of prophets so that there might be an unbroken succession of men who would proclaim Christ's coming. And to those prophets who would be most explicit (e.g. Isaiah, Daniel and Ezekiel) Christ himself would appear.

But with Solomon's slide into idolatry, things began to darken and, despite an outpouring of the Spirit in Ezra's day, the church generally declined into ignorant superstition. The lights of the types went out so that Christ the fulfilment might be seen as the only light: the temple was destroyed, the kings were removed; even prophecies eventually ceased as the time of the great prophet drew near. 'Thus the lights of the Old Testament go out on the approach of the glorious sun of righteousness.'[49]

But since the coming one would not just be the hope of Israel but the firstborn of the new creation, all creation went into labour to give him birth. History entered its most tumultuous stage as Babylon fell to Persia, Persia to Greece, and Greece to Rome. In those pagan empires, Satan was permitted to rise to his full strength in readiness for his final defeat. Also, heathen philosophy came to its height in Athens, permitted so that its insufficiency and the need for a divine teacher might be shown.

---

47. Ibid. p. 182.
48. Ibid. p. 210.
49. Ibid. p. 254.

At the same time the Jews began to be dispersed through the nations. This served to show the impracticality and so insufficiency of the temple's sacrificial system; more, it spread expectation of the Messiah through the world in preparation for the mass salvation of the Gentiles. And with some success, Edwards believed:

> Virgil the famous poet that lived in Italy a little before Christ was born, has a poem about the expectation of a great prince that was to be born and the happiness, time of righteousness and peace that he was to introduce, some of it very much in the language of the prophet Isaiah.[50]

The Scriptures were also translated into Greek, the language of the nations, 'making the facts concerning Jesus Christ publicly known through the world'.[51]

Thus the Old Testament (and, indeed, all world history) had prepared for the moment when Christ would come to purchase the redemption planned before creation itself.

Part 2: The purchase of redemption

Presumably, because the material is covered elsewhere, Edwards is remarkably brief in this second part, and its feel is much less historical and more abstract as he considers what Christ accomplished.

All Christ had done before his incarnation had been to prepare for this moment, but he could not actually redeem humans without becoming one of them himself. But from the moment of

---

50. Ibid. p. 257, referring to Virgil's *Fourth Eclogue* (something C. S. Lewis made a regular part of his Christmas reading). Through his life, Edwards became increasingly interested in the idea that the truths of the gospel had, in ancient times (especially Noah's day), been disseminated throughout the cultures of the world, there to be slowly distorted. See, for instance, Miscellany 1181, 'Traditions of the heathen, particularly the Chinese, concerning the Trinity, the nature of the Deity, the paradisaic state, the Fall, the redemption of the Messiah, the fall of angels, the nature of true religion' (*Works of Jonathan Edwards*, vol. 23, pp. 95–104).

51. *Works of Jonathan Edwards*, vol. 9, p. 258.

his conception, Christ began to purchase redemption. That meant humiliation, even from his birth, since while Mary and Joseph 'were both of the royal family of David, the most honorable family, and Joseph the rightful heir, yet the family was reduced to a very low state'.[52] And it meant almost immediate suffering, in his circumcision. Yet all this was necessary, for it was by such humiliation and suffering, even from conception, that he fulfilled the demands of the law and the covenant of works: 'the blood that was shed in his circumcision was propitiatory blood; but as it was a conformity to the law of Moses it was part of his meritorious righteousness'.[53]

It all culminated, of course, in the cross.

> Then was finished all that was required in order to satisfy the
> threatenings of the law, all in order to satisfy divine justice, the utmost
> that vindictive justice demanded, [the] whole debt paid. Then finished
> the whole of the purchase of eternal life.[54]

Part 3: From Pentecost to Christ's return
The last section looks at the subsequent spreading of that redemption through the world. Edwards held that God works in history primarily through extraordinary outpourings of his Spirit in revival. Thus he depicts the advance of Christ's kingdom happening in four great steps of awakening. Each time involves a growing degeneracy and opposition to the gospel; then God acts in judgment, the church is delivered and multitudes receive new life.

The first great step began with Christ's work on earth and ended with the destruction of Jerusalem in AD 70. In demolishing the temple (and so its whole sacrificial system), God thus judged the faithless Jews who were trusting in the types rather than their fulfilment. So redemption spread ever more to the Gentiles.

The second step involved the conversion of the Roman

52. Ibid. p. 300.

53. Ibid. pp. 307–308. For the 'covenant of works', see p. 97, on John Owen, in this book.

54. *Works of Jonathan Edwards*, vol. 9, p. 331.

emperor Constantine. This, Edwards is prepared to say, was 'the greatest revolution and change in the face of things on the face of the earth that ever came to pass in the world since the flood'.[55] Why? Because through it, pagan Rome, which had so oppressed the church, was destroyed. That effectively meant judgment on the entire heathen world, a judgment that was followed by the gospel being taken to such far countries as India and Ireland.

The third step concerns the destruction of papal Rome, an event so significant that the 'bigger part of the book of Revelation is taken up in foretelling the events of this period'.[56] After the conversion of Constantine, Satan succeeded in two great works: in the eastern half of the old Roman Empire he raised up Islam; in the western half he established the kingdom of Antichrist. Seated on seven hills, drunk with the blood of the saints, this of course was the Roman papacy.[57] But in the Reformation the fall of Antichrist began.

It all meant that it could not be long before Satan's kingdom was overthrown. And Edwards saw his own ministry to the Indians as proof of that. Satan, he believed, had first brought people to America so as to get them out of the reach of the gospel. But with the evangelization of even these remote people, it was clear that the ends of the earth were soon to be converted. He suggested that in their death throes Antichrist and Islam would make a final alliance against the church, only to be swiftly defeated. Then would come a time of unprecedented revival: 'the word of God shall have a speedy and swift progress through the earth';[58] Jew and heathen would convert en masse; then the earth, full of the knowledge of the Lord, would enjoy a thousand years of peace and prosperity.

Then (after a final apostasy) would come the fourth step in

---

55. Ibid. p. 396.

56. Ibid. p. 404.

57. Since the early days of the Reformation, it had been conventional for Protestant theologians to identify papal Rome as the persecuting whore of Babylon depicted in the book of Revelation.

58. *Works of Jonathan Edwards*, vol. 9, p. 466.

which Christ would return. In fact, the first three steps were all types of this one, for now Christ would judge the whole world and, not just spiritually now, but physically bring multitudes to new life. Then 'Christ's church shall forever leave this accursed world to go into that more glorious world, the highest heavens'; the world will be burned up, and the 'miserable company of wicked shall be left behind to have their cursed future executed upon 'em here'.[59]

There is undoubtedly material here that is problematic (e.g. the idea that this world is effectively to be discarded, not renewed); and yet we should probably be especially wary of our own re-actions at this point. It is all too easy to snigger snobbishly when Edwards so directly connects events in his own day to events in Revelation. Those links might have been wrong, but our reaction reveals something much more worrying in us. That is, we moderns instinctively find it incredible that 'real' secular history should ever be connected to, let alone be driven by, God's cosmic plan of re-demption. Edwards, on the other hand, rejected such dualism. He, at least, had a robustly Christian understanding of all history.[60]

The Harmony of the Old and New Testaments

This, Edwards's other projected 'great work', would, he said, have examined in more detail first, the Old Testament prophecies of the Messiah; secondly, Old Testament types of the gospel; and thirdly, 'the harmony of the Old and New Testament, as to doctrine and precept'.[61] Clearly, these were significant issues for Edwards, and yet, after a look at *A History of the Work of Redemption*, we probably have a good enough sense of where Edwards would have gone with this work. It would be made even more clear that the Old Testament is 'full of the gospel of Christ', and that 'Christ and his redemption are the great subject of the whole Bible'.[62]

---

59. Ibid. p. 505.

60. And not just history: his scientific notebooks (Ibid. vol. 6), for example, show how, even in the tiniest atomic details, Edwards refused to separate theology from the natural world and the discipline of science.

61. *Works of Jonathan Edwards*, vol. 16, p. 728.

62. Ibid. vol. 9, pp. 289–290.

That said, the question of types that he said he would examine here was more fundamental to Edwards than we have been able to see so far. For, the frequency with which God employed types in the Old Testament convinced Edwards that types were a regular means God used to communicate spiritual truths – and not just in Scripture. Indeed, Edwards held that since God had created in order to communicate himself, material reality naturally expressed and reflected the more substantial spiritual realities. Creation, he held, is a projection of the divine mind, and as such is entirely harmonious with the Creator, meaning that it is 'full of images of divine things, as full as a language is of words'.[63] To take one vital example: Edwards thought of the three persons of the Trinity con-stituting 'the supreme harmony of all';[64] their harmony provides the logic for all created harmony, such that singing in harmony (some-thing Edwards loved to do with his family) reflects divine beauty:

> The best, most beautiful, and most perfect way that we have of
> expressing a sweet concord of mind to each other, is by music. When
> I would form in my mind an idea of a society in the highest degree
> happy, I think of them as expressing their love, their joy, and the inward
> concord and harmony and spiritual beauty of their souls by sweetly
> singing to each other.[65]

All this meant that, out walking amidst trees and rivers, Edwards would continue being instructed in and reminded of the gospel. The tiniest details around him poured forth knowledge. How he came to recognize these types in creation was controlled essen-tially by Scripture: when, for example, he observed that the 'rising and setting of the sun is a type of the death and resurrection of Christ' he was working from scriptural ideas of the Light of the World, the Sun of Righteousness and broader themes of light and darkness.[66] That said, he did not believe that Scripture listed every

---

63. Ibid. vol. 11, p. 152.
64. Ibid. vol. 13, p. 329.
65. Ibid. p. 331.
66. Ibid. vol. 11, p. 64.

type to be found in creation; rather, it taught the principles. So, for example, he could suggest that 'Children's coming into the world naked and filthy, and in their blood, and crying and impotent, is to signify the spiritual nakedness, pollution of nature and wretchedness of condition with which they are born.'[67]

Edwards's writings are remarkable for how richly (and how well) he illustrates his points by describing similar things in creation. Yet he did not believe that he was inventing his illustrations; it was rather that creation was specifically designed to represent truths about the Creator and his work of redemption. God's being and all his ways, thought Edwards, are a harmony.

Going on with Edwards

You should be able to feel quite relaxed about where to set off in Edwards's works. He is generally quite easy-going. An obvious starting point is *Religious Affections*, a work that leaves no reader unchanged. But if that feels too lengthy, you can get a swift taste of the same brew in 'A Divine and Supernatural Light' or 'Distinguishing Marks of a Work of the Spirit of God'. A little trickier is *The End for Which God Created the World*, but you can avoid the harder bits and get much the same reward by diving straight into chapter 2.

Banner of Truth provide *Religious Affections* and *A History of the Work of Redemption* (among a number of his other works) as handy, stand-alone books; they also produce a two-volume *Works of Jonathan Edwards*, which is the cheapest way to own all his most essential writings and sermons. It is not comprehensive, though, and if you find yourself really wanting to get stuck into Edwards, there is nothing to rival the definitive *Works of Jonathan Edwards*, 26 vols. (New Haven: Yale University Press, 1957–2008). You needn't break the bank, however: everything can be read online for free at Yale University's Jonathan Edwards Center (http://edwards.yale. edu). I say 'read', but perhaps 'sampled' might be better: reading

67. Ibid. p. 54.

Edwards's major works on a computer screen would be as harsh as licking caviar off an old sock.

There is one other 'must read': George Marsden's *Jonathan Edwards: A Life* (New Haven: Yale University Press, 2003). Gripping, insightful; bluntly, unsurpassable.

Jonathan Edwards timeline

1703   Edwards born in East Windsor, Connecticut
1716   Begins studies at Yale College
1721   Conversion experience
1722   Assistant pastor in New York City; writes 'Resolutions'
1723   Pastor in Bolton, Connecticut
1724   Tutor at Yale
1727   Assistant pastor in Northampton; marries Sarah Pierpont
1729   Solomon Stoddard dies; Edwards becomes senior pastor
1734–5 Revival in Northampton
1739   Preaches *A History of the Work of Redemption*
1740   George Whitefield sparks second revival in Northampton
1741   Edwards preaches 'Sinners in the Hands of an Angry God'
1746   Publishes *Religious Affections*
1747   David Brainerd visits and dies in Edwards's home
1750   Dismissed as pastor of Northampton
1751   Pastor of Stockbridge mission station
1755   Writes *The End for Which God Created the World*
1758   Installed as president of the College of New Jersey (now Princeton University); dies

5. THE FATHER OF MODERN THEOLOGY

Friedrich Schleiermacher

On 14 July 1789 an angry mob surged into the courtyard of the Bastille prison in Paris, sparking off the French Revolution. But the revolution and its reign of terror were only the most violent expressions of a general mood of the age against God and his appointed kings and authorities. Here was a generation profoundly grateful to all those philosophers who gave them grounds for religious scepticism. Then into the breach stepped the imposing intellectual figure of Friedrich Schleiermacher, who, with impressive artistry, set out to reconcile the Spirit of Christianity with the spirit of his generation.

Strangely enough, Schleiermacher himself remains largely unknown to English speakers, and yet his impact was such that we can hardly do theology today without his presence all around us. The day after he died, August Neander, Professor of Theology at the University of Berlin, said to his students, 'From him a new period in the history of the church will one day take its origin.' He was right, and that day did not take long to arrive. The spirit of Schleiermacher presided over so much of the nineteenth century, and soon it was clear that a new era in theology had begun: the era of liberalism.

Given Schleiermacher's status as the father of liberalism, one would expect him to be a magnet for the wrath of the conservatives. In fact, though, Schleiermacher was so Christ-centred in his thought that even conservatives have struggled to know quite what to make of him. 'He gave up everything that he might save Christ' is the sort of awkward praise heard instead of outright condemnation. Charles Hodge, that bastion of nineteenth-century Princeton conservatism, wrote that when he was in Berlin he often attended Schleiermacher's church. And the hymns sung there, he said,

> were always evangelical and spiritual in an eminent degree, filled with praise and gratitude to our Redeemer . . . [and] Schleiermacher, when sitting in the evening with his family, would often say, 'Hush, children; let us sing a hymn of praise to Christ.' Can we doubt that he is singing those praises now? To whomsoever Christ is God, St. John assures us, Christ is a Saviour.[1]

Certainly Schleiermacher loved Jesus; of that there can be no doubt. However, he was a deeply complex and original thinker, and it will take some more wrestling with him before we can discern whether or not he really thought of Christ as the living God. But Schleiermacher is worth the wrestle! In fact, dear reader, you should guard yourself now against the temptation to dismiss him with anything like disdainful swagger. Schleiermacher was a giant among theologians, and his influence upon the church has been immense. To ignore through haughtiness or impatience the persuasive power of his theology will mean failure to understand his legacy as it surrounds us today.

Schleiermacher's life

Fritz Schleiermacher, as his friends called him, was born in 1768 in Breslau (then part of the Kingdom of Prussia, now Wroclaw in

---

1. C. Hodge, *Systematic Theology* (1871–3; repr. London: James Clarke, 1960), vol. 2, p. 440, n.

southern Poland). For generations, the men on both sides of his family had been Reformed preachers, and true to form his father Gottlieb became an army chaplain (though Freemasonry seems to have been dearer to his heart than the tenets of Calvinism).

Then, when Fritz was nine, the family moved near a Herrnhuter community. It was to prove a great turning point. The Herrnhuters (or Moravians) were Pietists who believed in the necessity of a living faith in Jesus and who reacted against the dry orthodoxy of the day, where doctrines, they felt, were treated like dead butter-flies, only to be collected, codified and catalogued. Expelled from Moravia, they had been given shelter at Herrnhut on the lands of Count Niklaus Ludwig von Zinzendorf, who became their bishop. The Schleiermacher family were profoundly impressed by this joyful community of living faith: Gottlieb was converted; and Fritz too, loving the experiential emphasis, soon underwent what he later referred to as his birth into a 'higher life'.

It was a good thing Fritz liked the Herrnhuters, for his parents gave their children over to be educated by them; and with his mother's death soon after and his father constantly on the move with the army, he never saw them again. The Herrnhuters thus became his new family, and shaped him permanently. And while he grew ever more frustrated with their doctrinal rigidity, he would always feel that true religion could not simply be taught but had to be experienced. Later in life he would define himself, saying, 'I have become a Herrnhuter again, only of a higher order.'

A 'Herrnhuter *again* . . .' So first there had to be a parting of the ways. It all began with a secret philosophical club Schleiermacher began at school. There, influenced by philosophers such as Rousseau, he began to question and then reject some of the Herrnhuters' doctrinal essentials (divine punishment for sin, the substitutionary sacrifice of Christ on the cross, the eternal deity of the Son). Casting off these doctrinal chains, he felt he was getting closer to true Christianity, and yet the eternal Son's atoning sacrifice for sin was at the very heart of Herrnhuter piety: it could not be discarded without consequences. When he wrote to his father describing his new views, his father was so appalled he lashed out with the harshest rebukes and the father–son relationship broke down irretrievably.

Gottlieb did, however, agree for his son to go to the University of Halle, an establishment that would provide just the sort of atmosphere of free inquiry that Fritz longed to escape the Herrnhuter college for. Not that he would attend many of the lectures there: frustrated by their plodding mediocrity, he embarked on his own, vastly more challenging study projects. He immersed himself in the study of Kant, read large amounts of Plato and Aristotle, and found that he was beginning to work out an entirely original theology. The whole time at Halle he found quite depressing, though. His short, slight frame had never been in good health ever since his sister dropped him as a child and left him mildly hunched and misshapen; but now all the reclusive study really took its toll. And it wasn't just his health; his reading left him sceptical and his isolation left him lonely. All the social and spiritual warmth he had enjoyed with the Herrnhuters was gone.

Then, as was the custom of the time for a man in his position, he accepted a tutoring post in the aristocratic Prussian household of Count von Dohna at Schlobitten. And in the warmth of that large and happy family, the cold cynicism that had thrived in the ivory towers of Halle was melted away and feelings of love began to bud: love for Jesus, and a secret love for one of the young countesses. He was becoming a Herrnhuter again. He began preaching regularly and passionately, his sermons full of both moral challenge and Christ as our model and ideal. He said it was as if he had 'revelation from within', and it was by that intuition that his theology was now developing fast.

He left Schlobitten, took an assistant pastorate in Landsberg for a couple of years (where he grabbed every moment he could to read the pantheist philosopher Spinoza); then, in 1796, aged twenty-seven, he took up his first post of real responsibility, as chaplain of the large and dirty Charity Hospital in Berlin. For Schleiermacher, Berlin was a Prussian Eden, with salons overflowing with poets, philosophers and talk of Romanticism.[2] With

---

2. Romanticism, which was really more of a mood than a movement, was a
   reaction against the cold rationalism of the Enlightenment; it championed
   instead the individual and her feelings, self-expression, personal creativity

its good society and cultured repartee, it seemed to have the warmth of Herrnhut but with that longed-for 'higher order' of conversation.

It was also a world with little room for God. At least, it had little room for any God who might want to express himself in the world. Thus Schleiermacher came to write his first book, *On Religion: Speeches to Its Cultured Despisers*. In it he argued that true religion (of which Christianity is the highest form) is not about the dead letter of doctrine and the sort of historical events that Enlightenment scepticism pooh-poohed; it is about a living experience of the divine. In other words, Romantic 'cultured despisers of religion' need not trouble themselves with off-putting dogmas such as God and human immortality, for true religion was all about what it is to be human, about having an intuition, a feeling for the universe, a taste for the infinite. It was a vision of Christianity as the ideal for which Romanticism was really striving.

Thus Schleiermacher made his name, and thus he established the trajectory of his mature theology. But he also used language that he would later retreat from: he called the pantheist Spinoza a holy man filled with the Spirit, and spoke of the 'the World', 'the Universe' and 'the One' as the proper object of our pious adoration. Such pantheist language, he soon realized, would have to be softened.

In and out of the salons, Schleiermacher was naturally sociable and made easy and interesting company. Personally, though, he preferred to be with women. In fact, he once admitted to a female friend, he wished that he could be a woman (women, he felt, cherish feeling more). This led to some distinctly uncomfortable social situations, such as when, for example, he developed romantic attachments to two married women. One of them,

---

Foonote 2 (*cont.*)

and mystery. Hear the heroic self-expression in a Beethoven symphony; think of the dark, questioning mystery of Mary Shelley's *Frankenstein*, of Wordsworth swooning over the ruins of Tintern Abbey or Turner's brooding washes of paint as he depicts some shipwreck – then you feel the spirit of Romanticism.

Eleonore von Grunow, was in an unhappy marriage with a pastor, which Schleiermacher concluded could be no true marriage. So he courted and secretly betrothed himself to her. Seeing the difficulty, Bishop Sack sent Schleiermacher far away to a tiny parish in Stolpe on the Baltic coast.

His time in Stolpe was a sobering one after the heady Romanticism of Berlin, but it was not long before he was summoned to the University of Halle as Professor of Theology and University Preacher. There he got his first taste of lecturing on the New Testament – and on everything else on the syllabus bar the Old Testament. But even the Halle days weren't to last long. A couple of years later, in 1806, Napoleon's Grand Army were marching through the streets and the university was shut down amid city-wide chaos.

But from the smoke and carnage now rose a new and more fiery Schleiermacher. Seeing Napoleon as a demonic figure, the enemy of freedom, Schleiermacher channelled his energy into volcanic sermons of patriotic resistance. There is something fascinating about the way his red-blooded nationalism sits next to his self-consciously feminine sensitivity; but in any case it stirred all Prussia. In 1808 he was back in Berlin, and now the whole city throbbed with his emotive, charismatic preaching and optimistic vision of God on the side of Prussia (and his legacy would continue: he later prepared a young Otto von Bismarck for confirmation).

The real reason Schleiermacher returned to Berlin was to assume the eminent pastorate of Trinity Church, where for the rest of his life he would preach nearly every Sunday to a packed congregation. And dalliances with the ladies would not be a problem this time, for he came with only one in mind: Henriette von Willich, the widow of a friend and some twenty years his junior. Soon they were married and their house was as packed as the church (she brought two children from her first marriage and they had four more together).

There was one other major demand on his time in this, his mature and settled phase. It was the creation and establishment of the new University of Berlin, and Schleiermacher was one of its key architects. Once it had been formed, he served as dean for many years, rector for a while, and lectured each day during the week, teaching New Testament, doctrine, church history and almost every theological discipline except the Old Testament.

As the founder of the theological faculty, he got to write the syllabus and so outline his vision of theology. It was something he then mapped out in his highly illuminative *Brief Outline of the Study of Theology*. There Schleiermacher argues that theology should be divided into three basic disciplines. The first is philosophical theology, which, he argued, should basically define the essence of Christianity. The second is historical theology, which should describe how Christianity has been spoken of down through history. Perhaps most revealing of all, historical theology he believed should include exegesis, which is simply an examination of the very first expressions of Christian experience (in the New Testament) and doctrine, which is how Christian experience is expressed today. In other words, the New Testament and Christian doctrine are mere historical and cultural expressions of Christian experience. The third basic discipline he believed should be practical theology, which then applies what has been learnt in the other disciplines to the church today.

His health did decline during those productive years in Berlin, and he found himself seeking any number of alternative remedies, even consulting a spiritualist friend of his wife's who lodged with them. Still, though, the end came quickly when a severe case of pneumonia struck in February 1834. He called the household together to celebrate the Lord's Supper, and during that he died. It was a small family ceremony, but all Prussia was struck by the death of their national prophet, and tens of thousands would follow his casket through the streets of Berlin to the cemetery.

Schleiermacher's thought

Schleiermacher's interests were broad and extensive: he produced a definitive translation of Plato, preached innumerable sermons, wrote New Testament studies, manuals of hermeneutics, a systematic theology, a life of Jesus and a church history. But underneath all these lay one foundational concern. He wanted to restate the

Christian faith in such a way that traditional Christianity could be made both credible and relevant to the modern age. In other words, he was, before he was anything else, an apologist. Even the bedrock of his theology would be formed (as he put it) by 'propositions borrowed from apologetics'.

In practice this meant pulling Christianity back beyond the range of any rational attacks from the Enlightenment. Christianity would be about religious experience so exclusively that any Enlightenment scepticism over doctrinal or historical details would simply be rendered irrelevant. In this way, not only would Christianity become intellectually unassailable; it would become much more available to modern people who need no longer abandon any modern belief in becoming a Christian.

The Christian Faith
This, Schleiermacher's *chef d'oeuvre*, written at the height of his powers during his mature Berlin years, became the seminal statement of liberal Protestantism, and is commonly ranked alongside Calvin's *Institutes* as one of the most important works of Protestant theology. It is, without doubt, a true masterpiece, dazzling in its originality and quite beautifully composed. In complete contrast to those systematic theologies that lurch from disconnected doctrine to disconnected doctrine, *The Christian Faith* is a coherent and organic whole which clearly shows the interrelation of various doctrines. And just that changed how theology must be done: after Schleiermacher, systematic theologies that present doctrines in a disconnected way just seem clunky and naive.

The work opens with a vitally important introduction, which is essentially the recipe for all that follows. The ingredients are listed and the method to be pursued outlined. The First Part then explains what philosophical principles and general religious premises Christians must presuppose. The Second Part then builds more specifically Christian thought on the foundations shaped by those presuppositions.

Introduction
The root and origin of everything to follow is Schleiermacher's description of the essence of piety. It is, he said, 'the consciousness

of being absolutely dependent'.[3] He then proceeds to describe the history of humanity as the history of the development of this consciousness. Initially, this feeling of dependence was expressed only crudely through primitive fetishism and polytheism. But as religion developed it became more and more monotheistic until the religious impulse reached its zenith in Christianity.[4] Christianity, for Schleiermacher, is the purest form of monotheism and therefore the very highest stage of religious evolution. Judaism and Islam are weak approximations to the clean monotheism of Christianity, but are in themselves too bound up with the physical to be considered strictly monotheist (this is clearly not an argument that many Jews or Muslims, looking at the Trinity, would find very convincing). Schleiermacher was thus keen to distance Christianity from Judaism and Old Testament faith, for while he recognized Christianity has historical connections to the Old Testament, he believed that that faith was of a more primitive sort, with as much to do with Christianity as the philosophies of Plato and Aristotle (or perhaps less in practice).

In this history of religion there is no sharp distinction between true worship and idolatry. Instead, the religious instinct is a universally good thing, and simply expressed in different ways: 'we must never deny the homogeneity of all these products of the human spirit, but must acknowledge the same root even for the lower powers'.[5] The overall picture, then, is of a smooth, evolutionary

---

3. *The Christian Faith* (2nd ed. of *Der Christliche Glaube* [Berlin: Reimer, 1830–31]), ed. H. R. Mackintosh and J. S. Stewart (Edinburgh: T. & T. Clark, 1999), §4.

4. Schleiermacher's Berlin colleague, G. W. F. Hegel, quipped that if true religion really is simply the feeling of dependence, then 'the dog is the best Christian, for it has this most strongly . . . The dog also has feelings of redemption when its hunger is appeased by a bone' (quoted in K. Barth, *The Theology of Schleiermacher* [Grand Rapids: Eerdmans, 1982], p. 186). The critique is unfair, for while the dog may have feelings of dependence, those feelings would have to be of a higher and more developed order to qualify as specifically Christian.

5. Schleiermacher, *Christian Faith*, §8, postscript 1.

development of religion up to Christianity. Christianity here is the apogee of human searching, the ultimate civilization and triumph of the human spirit over nature.

It might seem surprising that Schleiermacher should have had a model of evolution so close to the heart of his system when writing a generation before Charles Darwin. However, Darwin's model of biological evolution emerged within an already existing evolutionary understanding of reality. One of Schleiermacher's colleagues at the University of Berlin was G. W. F. Hegel, the Professor of Philosophy, and a decade before Schleiermacher started compiling *The Christian Faith*, Hegel had put forth a massive argument for the evolutionary movement of all history towards – well, himself and his society.[6] Schleiermacher's model of the happy upward progress of religion thus sat well with the times.

It also dispensed nicely with any need for the supernatural. Christianity here was no longer so much about God intervening in salvation; it was more the culmination of a process. In fact, even the coming of Christ (what makes Christianity Christian) was for Schleiermacher more like an evolutionary step than God acting supernaturally in the world: Christ's purpose was 'gradually to quicken the entire human race into higher life'.[7]

The evolution model also set aside the problematic existence of so many different religions. For Schleiermacher, no longer were the different religions vying with each other to describe ultimate reality; all were simply expressions of the universal religious impulse. And though Christianity could be seen as the highest stage of religious evolution so far, it was not as if Christ is the final end of all. Even Christ might be superseded.

All this could be said by a Christian theologian because 'Christian doctrines are accounts of the Christian religious

---

6. 'Hegel's only real fault', wrote Robert Jenson, 'was that he confused himself with the last judge; but that is quite a fault' (R. W. Jenson, *The Knowledge of Things Hoped for: The Sense of Theological Discourse* [Oxford: Oxford University Press, 1969], p. 233).

7. *Christian Faith*, §13.1.

affections set forth in speech.'[8] (Courage, dear reader!) With this key affirmation we can see an intriguing similarity to Jonathan Edwards: both were writing in the face of Enlightenment critiques of Christianity, both rejected the idea that Christian belief could be boiled down to mere assent to a list of doctrines, and both emphasized the importance of experience and religious affections. But here Schleiermacher turned Edwards's theological universe on its head, for where Edwards believed that holy affections arise from doctrine, Schleiermacher argued that doctrines are the product of our religious affections. It was a true Copernican revolution in theology: religious affections were here moved to the central place previously occupied by divine revelation. They would now be the source of our theological knowledge. (And it takes hardly a moment's thought to see how completely Schleiermacher's revolution has triumphed today.)

For Schleiermacher, then, doctrine was not truth about (or from) God as such: God is in reality ineffable, and language about him could only then be a lisping attempt to describe indescribable reality. Instead, doctrine is a cultural expression of the deeper reality of religious consciousness, a communal attempt to communicate religious experience. But this was an entirely happy realization for Schleiermacher: no longer need Christians be divided by their doctrinal differences. They could be unreservedly ecumenical. And Schleiermacher was: Trinity Church in Berlin became a united Lutheran–Reformed congregation, and he worked and preached passionately for peace and unity in the Prussian church.

In all this, he was unswerving in his belief that he was upholding the Reformation in his day. His greatest Reformation hero was, unsurprisingly, Erasmus, the champion of doctrine–light unity. But he also spoke most highly of Calvin and his concern for religious affections. The very title *The Christian Faith* he thought of as an evangelical, Reformation statement, for he would be the theologian of 'faith alone'; that is, faith free of hard doctrine. He would focus on 'faith' as a thing in itself. Yet the result of this turn

---

8. Ibid. §15.

to examine 'faith' in itself was that, where the eye of the Reformers was outward to God's revelation of himself, Schleiermacher's faith was forced to be an essentially introspective thing.

First Part

Having established that course for his theology, Schleiermacher then sets out the more basic religious presuppositions that must underlie more specifically Christian experience.

He begins with creation. Or perhaps it would be more accurate to say he begins with the existence of the world, for 'we have no consciousness of a beginning of being'.[9] That is, while our 'feeling of absolute dependence' does speak of the world as having its origin in God, it is simply not able to go so far as to say whether or not the world had a beginning. Thus 'the controversy over the temporal or eternal creation of the world . . . has no bearing on the content of the feeling of absolute dependence, and it is therefore a matter of indifference how it is decided'.[10] And we need to have the same sort of agnosticism towards the existence of angels, who, he says, are not only irrelevant, but only seem to have made an appearance in the New Testament as a sort of hangover from the more primitive religion of the Old Testament. As for the Devil, that idea 'is so unstable that we cannot expect anyone to be convinced of its truth'.[11]

On, then, to the preservation of creation. Schleiermacher believed that a single, divine, eternal decree underlay the whole of creation. And, God being perfect, this decree so perfectly established creation that it exists without any need to depend on God in any direct, moment-by-moment way. Creation can operate like clockwork 'by the system of Nature'.[12] Furthermore, God being good, he has created a good universe, and as such there is no need for him ever to step in and correct things. What he created was good (and clearly nothing since – like a historical Fall of man – has

---

9. Ibid. §39.
10. Ibid. §41.2.
11. Ibid. §44.
12. Ibid. §47.

upset that). God, then, relates to the whole, but has no need to engage specifically with any individuals or any one part of creation. In fact, if he were to intervene or have any direct dealings with any particular part of creation, it would be an admission that he had not, in fact, created a good universe in the first place. No miracles, then, and no personal relationships with this God. (Cue the eerie sound of Luther, Calvin, Owen and Edwards turning ever faster in their graves.)

What then, asks Schleiermacher, can we learn about God from all this? (Given that God is ineffable and that doctrine is the product of our religious affections, Schleiermacher is of course unable to discuss the doctrine of God by itself. Instead, he spreads his doctrine of God throughout *The Christian Faith*, seeing what can be said about God from what is more immediately apparent to our 'feelings of dependence'.) The first thing to be said is that, since we feel absolutely dependent, God must be the absolute cause. And God being the cause of time and temporal being, he must therefore be eternal and absolutely above all time. But not just time: God causes all space, and thus must be omnipresent. In fact, he causes all that is finite, and thus must be infinite and therefore omnipotent. And since he causes all, he must know all and therefore must be omniscient. (There are some other less significant divine attributes, he informs us, but for now they can only be inferred from those more immediately obvious ones.)

Second Part
The remainder of the work is shaped around the themes of sin and grace (the examination of grace being where the overall argument finally becomes most explicitly Christian).

Sin, first of all, is essentially God-forgetfulness. It is the failure to have that 'feeling of absolute dependence', and is therefore the attempt to feel independent. But as I feel independent, I am simply deluding myself, imagining that somehow I am truly the author of my own existence. Forgetting God, then, renders me ignorant of myself (the knowledge of God and self being intertwined: one can hear Calvin's influence coming through clearly). And it renders me not only ignorant: thinking I am independent makes me feel unsupported and vulnerable. Thus scared and isolated, I begin to see myself in competition with others. Fearful, deluded and selfish: this is the 'flesh'.

Schleiermacher chose to open his examination of sin by looking at sin in us today, and this for good reason, since he did not believe in a historical fall of Adam. That the smooth progress of history could have been interrupted by a cataclysmic event that altered the very nature of the physical world had to be pure fantasy. Yet Schleiermacher wanted to affirm his belief in some sort of idea of original sin. What it could not mean was that sin and guilt are somehow inherited or received from some external source. How, exactly, could God-forgetfulness be inherited? It had to be that, since we are nurtured in a God-forgetful society, so we become forgetful of God ourselves.

Jettisoning belief in a historical Fall turned out to be a more significant step than Schleiermacher had perhaps first realized, though, and he quickly found himself struggling to account for sin. He would say, for instance, 'We are conscious of sin as the power and work of a time when the disposition to God-consciousness had not yet actively emerged in us,' which fitted the evolutionary progression idea well, but did this mean that our natural, created state was sinful?[13] His answer could only be confusing: sin's 'existence does not invalidate the idea of the original perfection of man, still we are bound to regard it as a derangement of our nature'.[14]

Next Schleiermacher turns to evil, which is the result of and punishment for sin. Evil is all about that sinful loss of God-consciousness. Something is evil when God is forgotten. But as such, evil is something that is relative: my family could be killed in a car crash, but if that did not disturb my God-consciousness, it would not be an evil. Only if the accident caused me to forget God would it be an evil. That being the case, God can be described as the author of evil in just the same way as he is the author of good, since those things we perceive as evil are only evil for us because of our God-forgetfulness. (Perhaps unsurprisingly, Schleiermacher

---

13. Ibid. §67.
14. Ibid. §68.

never ventures to discuss moral evil.) Our duty, then, is not to seek an end to evil as such, but an end to our God-forgetfulness.

What then, asks Schleiermacher, can we learn about God from this? First, it is clear that we need redemption, and thus we can say that God is holy. And since he ordains that evil be the consequence for sin, he must be just. Is he merciful, though? Here Schleiermacher gets distinctly nervous, because mercy implies God having a personal feeling and response, and such, he says, would be unworthy of God.

He moves instead to talk of his second major theme: grace. Grace, he argues, comes to us in much the same way as sin comes to us. That is, just as we forget God as a result of being reared in a God-forgetful society, so we can be brought to fresh consciousness of God in a God-conscious society. In a community of God-consciousness (the church) we can be weaned from God-forgetfulness and a new principle of God-consciousness can be infused into us.

But where has this community of God-consciousness come from? Ultimately, from Christ, and Schleiermacher now turns to considering him. Christ, he sees, was a man with perfect God-consciousness. In fact, this is the sense in which we can say God was 'in him': 'The Redeemer, then, is like all men in virtue of the identity of human nature, but distinguished from them all by the constant potency of His God-consciousness, which was a veritable existence of God in Him.'[15] Christ, then, was not the pre-existent and eternal Son, but a perfectly pious man – in effect, he was the first Christian. Not God become man but man become godly. Schleiermacher was quite aware that his view would entail a complete re-evaluation of the church's traditional teaching on the person of Christ. But he was eager for that. It would mean that off-putting and irrelevant doctrines could be stripped away, doctrines such as the virgin birth for which his system could find 'virtually no trace of a dogmatic purpose'.[16] In fact, if Christ's mere consciousness of God could amount to the very existence of God

---

15. Ibid. §94; cf. §99, postscript.
16. Ibid. §97.2.

in him, then even the doctrine of a personal God would have to be reformed completely.

Reeling from all that, it is easy to miss what is perhaps the biggest shock here. In everything, Schleiermacher has deliberately pursued a theology that is the product of religious affections. But now, at the heart of it all and underlying the very possibility of our having the God-consciousness we should have is this historically objective person. So which is it to be? An external redemption accomplished in history, or internal affections? Either our religious affections really are the source of all our doctrine (in which case the historical appearance of Christ has no place here and has been smuggled in illegitimately) or there are such things as objective historical and therefore doctrinal facts.

But back to Christ's God-consciousness. It was for him, says Schleiermacher, a state of such 'unclouded blessedness' that he could experience no evil.[17] Pain and suffering did not trouble him, nor could anything weaken his God-consciousness. (Christ's agony in Gethsemane and his cry of dereliction on the cross were moments Schleiermacher preferred to soften, if soften is the word.) And Christ's work of redemption consisted precisely in the impartation of this God-consciousness to others. 'Indeed, Christ's highest achievement consists in this, that He so animates us that we ourselves are led to an ever more perfect fulfilment of the divine will.'[18]

Clearly redemption, for Schleiermacher, is much more about the God-consciousness of Christ during his life than it is about his death. The idea of Christ as a substitutionary sacrifice on the cross is entirely rejected. What, then, of the cross? It was the moment when Christ proved that, come what may, his God-consciousness would not falter. 'His blessedness emerged in its perfect fulness only in that it was not overcome even in the full tide of suffering.'[19] Thus when we see Christ on the cross we can only be impressed by his blessedness and so be drawn into it ourselves.

----

17. Ibid. §101.
18. Ibid. §104.3.
19. Ibid. §101.4.

Schleiermacher deliberately omitted the resurrection and ascension, arguing that they are not integral parts of the Christian faith. Though he does not say as much here, this was almost certainly connected to his doubts as to whether Jesus really died on the cross. Schleiermacher leaned towards the idea that Jesus only seemed dead, but was then taken down and revived.

One cannot really speak of God's mighty acts of salvation here, but once again this all fits Schleiermacher's story of the steady evolution of man. It is not even an evolutionary jump that Christ brings about, for his God-consciousness is really only a more potent version of something we all have. It is more that Christ is an enabler, pulling us up to a more perfect or complete stage in the history of humanity. Schleiermacher speaks of Christ as the redeemer, but since there is no Fall to be redeemed from, perhaps it would capture his thought more accurately to speak of Christ here as our perfecter.

Something else worth spotting about Christ's God-consciousness here is that it does not really amount to a personal relationship with God. That is not, after all, something Schleiermacher sees as being possible with God. The result is that Christ himself begins to look more like a principle than a person (perhaps we shouldn't be too surprised, given how awkward the presence of a historical person is in this system). Christ's kingly office, for example, is not portrayed as being anything to do with his personal rule; it 'consists in the fact that everything which the community of believers requires for its well-being continually proceeds from Him'.[20] It is as if Christ could be a pleasant smell, imparting to us, not a relationship, but the universal presence of the Infinite.

Next Schleiermacher turns to look at the effects the grace of Christ has on believers. Above and beyond anything else, of course, redemption for the individual will mean being brought to share in Christ's God-consciousness and blessedness. Regeneration is finding our God-consciousness awoken; sanctification is the deepening of that God-consciousness. But Schleiermacher also talks

---

20. Ibid. §105.

about our justification. Justification, for Schleiermacher, clearly cannot mean anything like a divine declaration that I, personally, am now righteous before God. God does not deal with individuals like that. No, God has 'only one eternal and universal decree justifying men for Christ's sake'.[21] Justification is an eternal decree for humanity as a whole. So my own justification must be about my appropriation of that decree to myself.

But what could that mean? With complete consistency, Schleiermacher has asserted that there is no such thing as divine wrath: such a primitive idea suggests an irritable (personal) God. In fact, there does not seem to be such a thing as actual sin and actual guilt; it is simply that we sense these things. We have been created good, after all, and merely perceive guilt in order that we might be spurred on to do better. Forgiveness of sins, then, cannot be about God forgiving me, but about my conscience being cleansed from guilt (though it is hard to see quite how this could work and what pastoral comfort it could give when guilt is not real and there is no actual divine pardon to be had).

His readers' nerves notwithstanding, on moves Schleiermacher then to reconceive the church. The church, he feels, began when Christ influenced his disciples with his blessedness and so established a community of God-consciousness. The disciples then influenced others, so becoming the foundations of a new community where, instead of sharing our God-forgetfulness, as happens elsewhere, we share our God-consciousness. This community, being about the perfection of human God-consciousness, is the future of humanity, and as such must be an ever-expanding community that will one day include all, even if only after death: 'everyone still outside this fellowship will some time or another be laid hold of by the divine operations of grace and brought within it'.[22]

Importantly, Schleiermacher now introduces us to the Spirit – the Spirit which once so filled the man Jesus of Nazareth, and which is now the common spirit of this new community. This Spirit is not a person or even a supernatural force; indeed, this

---

21. Ibid. §109.3.
22. Ibid. §118.1.

Spirit is now 'no longer personally operative in any individual, but henceforth manifests itself actively in the fellowship of believers as their common spirit'.[23] In other words, the Spirit is the common disposition to God-consciousness that the community of the church shares. This Spirit is what binds the community together, undoing the isolation of sin and so making us more perfectly human, as we were created to be.

In this new community we foster each other's God-consciousness particularly through the witness of the New Testament and preaching Christ. 'Faith comes from preaching' he says with all the resolve of a traditional evangelical.[24] For it is when we remember Christ's blessedness that we desire to be rid of our God-forgetfulness. But why open the New Testament rather than simply share our religious affections? It was not that the New Testament needed to be reliable or authoritative; it was that it records the experience of the earliest Christians, and thus influences and inspires us. The New Testament does these things, but of course the Old Testament, as the expression of a legalistic, pre-Christian faith, could not. 'Even the noblest Psalms always contain something which Christian piety is unable to appropriate as a perfectly pure expression of itself.'[25] Thus Schleiermacher considered the Old Testament 'a superfluous authority'.[26]

After then explaining how we are received into the church through baptism and regularly strengthened by remembering Christ in the Lord's Supper, he comes to a revealing analysis of prayer. Given all that he has said about how God does not interact with or deal with individuals, we should not be surprised to read his warning against petitionary prayer. Praise is appropriate, but we cannot think that we can affect or interact with God. Petition should be reserved for our fellow men, particularly fellow believers, that they might be united, and Schleiermacher ends with a passionate appeal for church unity.

---

23. Ibid. §124.2.
24. Ibid. §121.2.
25. Ibid. §132.2.
26. Ibid. §27.3; cf. §12.

Before moving on, though, Schleiermacher inserted an important appendix to this section on the church. In it he argues that, while there have been people who have shared their God-consciousness with each other ever since the beginning of the human race, the church began with the man Jesus of Nazareth. 'Christ could not have exerted any redeeming influence' on any who lived before him – in fact, he could not have exerted it on those, such as Simeon, who knew him only as a child.[27] Schleiermacher realized that he was stepping out on a limb here:

> The Confessions [the creeds and confessions of orthodox faith] . . .
> assume that faith in Christ existed before His personal action [the
> incarnation], but we make such faith conditional on, and derive it from,
> His personal action.[28]

His suggestion was that before the incarnation, instead of trusting Christ, people trusted in promises. And those promises were necessarily vague. Indeed, had they been specific, Christ need not have come; all he brought through the incarnation would already have been made clear through the promises.

Schleiermacher's last main subject for discussion is what he calls 'the consummation of the church'. He chose his words carefully, for he would now take language usually understood as referring to future events and explain how really they are 'a pattern to which we have to approximate'.[29] The fact is, if doctrine is an expression of our own experience, then we cannot speak of the future, since we have no experience of it. Schleiermacher maintained that we can make only logical inferences about the future. For example, we can deduce that the notion of eternal damnation is a false one, since it is incompatible with the eternal blessedness that Christ is disseminating throughout humanity.

How, then, should we understand such New Testament ideas as the return of Christ? Not literally. Rather, it is essentially about

---

27. Ibid. §156.1.
28. Ibid.
29. Ibid. §157.

'the reunion of believers with Christ'.[30] And that is both a present and a future experience. The last judgment, similarly, is about the separation of the church from the world. What we can vaguely sense, though, is that, since the infinite and immortal divine unites with the human in Christ, there must be some sort of continuation for us beyond death, even an 'organic life which has links of attachment to our present state'.[31] Then we will share Christ's 'unclouded blessedness' (though, given that Christ's 'unclouded blessedness' included having nowhere to lay his head, thirst, tiredness and the cross, this is probably not a fate that will excite every Christian).

Finally, asks Schleiermacher, what can we learn about God from this whole understanding of the theme of grace? Essentially, what we have seen is that 'the Supreme Being imparts Himself', and thus we can conclude that he is wise (so arranging things that he can impart himself) and loving.[32] It seems rather ambitious to equate something imparting itself with love (after all, the smell of sewage can impart itself), but then this is the tightrope Schleiermacher tries to walk: he wants to speak of God as loving, but not as personal.

Talk of God's love brings us at the very last to the Trinity, 'the coping-stone of Christian doctrine'.[33] Having seen 'the union of the Divine Essence with human nature, both in the personality of Christ and in the common Spirit of the Church', we can conclude that we experience God as a Trinity.[34] That is not to say that Schleiermacher thought of Father, Son and Spirit as three divine persons: the Spirit, certainly, is not a person, and the idea of personhood generally, he felt, impugned God's infinity.

The result is a discussion of the Trinity that looks like a rather incongruous and useless third nipple on the torso of his overall system and understanding of God. And it is so because Schleiermacher's God is fundamentally impersonal and

---

30. Ibid. §160.2.
31. Ibid. §161.3.
32. Ibid. §166.1.
33. Ibid. §170.1.
34. Ibid.

non-relational. He does not interact with us, and we cannot interact with him. Schleiermacher asserts that 'the consciousness of being absolutely dependent' is the same thing as being in relation with God.[35] But is it? I am dependent on air, but I don't have a relationship with air in the same way I have a relationship with my wife, or even my dog (on whom I do not depend). Talk of the love of the Father for the Son, the love of God for the world or our love for God simply cannot arise from the system of *The Christian Faith*.

But once again, Schleiermacher knew he was reinventing traditional Christianity for his time. He was quite prepared to admit that the Trinity was something of an appendix for him. He was eager to question conventional ideas, such as

> that both the Second and the Third Person in the Trinity were implicated even in the creation of the world, while the Second Person was also the subject thereafter of all the Old Testament theophanies, and it was from the Third Person that the whole prophetic movement of the Old Testament received its impulse.[36]

For, while he felt he must speak of the Trinity at the end of *The Christian Faith*, he was quite consciously striving for 'a thoroughgoing criticism of the doctrine in its older form'.[37] In fact, the 'position assigned to the doctrine of the Trinity in the present work is perhaps at all events a preliminary step towards this goal'.[38]

Going on with Schleiermacher

Schleiermacher is not an easy (or, ironically, heart-warming) read. But still he is usually less painful to approach than the bulk of the secondary literature on him, which tends to be extraordinarily

---

35. Ibid. §4.
36. Ibid. §170.3.
37. Ibid. §172.2.
38. Ibid. §172.3.

dusty and confusing. *The Christian Faith* (ed. H. R. Mackintosh and J. S. Stewart) is still in print (2nd ed. of *Der Christliche Glaube* [Berlin: Reimer, 1830–31]; Edinburgh: T. & T. Clark, 1999); and Keith Clements's *Friedrich Schleiermacher: Pioneer of Modern Theology* (London: Collins, 1987) provides a useful selection of some other key texts, along with a good introduction and notes.

Two other books worth pursuing are J. Gresham Machen's *Christianity and Liberalism* (New York: Macmillan, 1923), an almost painfully penetrating critique of Schleiermacher's liberal heritage; and from the opposite point of view, James Barr's *Fundamentalism* (London: SCM, 1977) is an equally thought-provoking condemnation of conservative theology for, among other things, what Barr sees as an almost universal capitulation to Schleiermacher's legacy.

Friedrich Schleiermacher timeline

1760	Count Niklaus von Zinzendorf dies
1768	Schleiermacher born in Breslau (modern Wroclaw, Poland)
1770	G. W. F. Hegel born
1776	American Revolution
1783–7	Attends Herrnhuter schools at Niesky and Barby
1787–9	University at Halle
1789	French Revolution
1790–93	Tutor to von Dohna family in Schlobitten
1794–6	Assistant pastor in Landsberg
1796–1801	Chaplain, Charity Hospital, Berlin
1799	*On Religion: Speeches to Its Cultured Despisers*
1802–4	Pastor in Stolpe
1804–6	Professor of Theology, University of Halle
1806	Napoleon Bonaparte invades Prussia
1808	Pastor of Trinity Church, Berlin
1809	Marries Henriette von Willich; Professor of Theology, University of Berlin
1811	*Brief Outline of the Study of Theology*
1821–2	*The Christian Faith*
1834	Schleiermacher dies

6. THE BOMBSHELL IN THE PLAYGROUND OF THE THEOLOGIANS

Karl Barth

Karl Barth towers above the theological landscape of today. Is it just because he is so close to us in time that he seems so titanic? Certainly, it is harder to be objective about a giant close-up, but either way he was a giant, dominating the theology of the last century. And, like all giants, Barth scares people: the thirteen hefty volumes that make up his colossal (but unfinished!) main work, the *Church Dogmatics*, are enough to send most people scurrying for the secondary literature or some sound bite by which to understand him. Thus you hear Barth described as 'neo-orthodox', or some such tag. The tags are usually neither accurate nor helpful. And yet, scared of approaching Barth himself, slogans are often all that students are left with. In fact, it is not just the students: even the most respected theologians have been known to have created Barths of their own imagining. This was something that clearly frustrated the man himself:

> Am I deceived when I have the impression that I exist in the phantasy of far too many . . . mainly, only in the form of certain, for the most part hoary, summations of certain pictures hastily dashed off by some

person at some time, and for the sake of convenience, just as hastily
accepted, and then copied endlessly, and which, of course, can easily be
dismissed?[1]

He had good reason to feel unjustly dealt with, for he himself was
capable of highly respectful and intricate readings of those with
whom he disagreed (such as Friedrich Schleiermacher).

Who, then, was this colossus?

Barth's life

In 1886 Karl Barth was born in Basel, Switzerland, to a family of
pastors who, unusually for the times, were by and large theologic-
ally conservative. Tensions quickly developed then, when, aged
eighteen, he set off to Germany to study under the greatest liberal
theologians of the day: Adolf von Harnack in Berlin and Wilhelm
Herrmann in Marburg. Before long he was known as a rising star
of liberalism, and though he would soon utterly renounce that theology, those years were influential. Herrmann especially, who was
very much a disciple of Schleiermacher, profoundly affected Barth
with his transparently genuine and profound love for Jesus.

His studies completed, he moved to become an assistant pastor
in Geneva, and there plunged into Calvin's *Institutes* for the first
time. He even found himself preaching from Calvin's old pulpit,
though later he would write, 'I'm afraid Calvin would hardly have
been very pleased at the sermons which I preached in his pulpit
then'.[2] But it was only a few years later, after he had become the
pastor of the little village of Safenwil, between Zurich and Bern,
that the wheels really began to come off his liberalism. Telling
people to be religious, it was becoming clear, was not helping them.

---

1. Karl Barth, 'Foreword to the English Translation', in Otto Weber, *Karl Barth's Church Dogmatics* (London: Lutterworth, 1953), p. 7.
2. Letter to F. J. Leenhardt, 14 February 1959, cited in E. Busch, *Karl Barth: His Life from Letters and Autobiographical Texts* (Philadelphia: Fortress; SCM: London, 1976), pp. 53–54.

Then, in 1914, war broke out, and Barth was shocked to find his liberal teachers supporting it. All his confidence in them and their theology was rocked as he saw their total accommodation of the gospel to the culture. And so 'I gradually turned back to the Bible', and found a 'strange new world' there. As with Luther, it began with Romans: in the summer of 1916, 'I sat under an apple tree and began to apply myself to Romans with all the resources that were available to me at the time . . . I began to read it as though I had never read it before.'[3] It forced him to repudiate all his old theological inheritance and reach out for a new way of thinking.

The notes he made on Romans were published early in 1919, and immediately caused outrage. And no wonder: instead of the old liberal, critical method of filtering the text through the dust of a historically reconstructed context, Barth wanted to use 'the old doctrine of Verbal Inspiration' and let the text speak directly.[4] It was with this cheek that he began:

> Paul, as a child of his age, addressed his contemporaries. It is, however, far more important that, as Prophet and Apostle of the Kingdom of God, he veritably speaks to all men of every age. The differences between then and now, there and here, no doubt require careful investigation and consideration. But the purpose of such investigation can only be to demonstrate that these differences are, in fact, purely trivial.[5]

So what Paul said about Jewish attitudes to the law, for example, applied to the liberal view of religiosity. That is, liberalism treated religiosity as a ladder to God. Without any help from God, liberalism believed, we can speak of and know him.

In place of all that, Barth increasingly wanted to argue that there is in reality a 'dialectical' relationship between God and humanity.

---

3. K. Barth, *The Theology of Schleiermacher* (Grand Rapids: Eerdmans, 1982), p. 264.

4. K. Barth, *The Epistle to the Romans* (London: Oxford University Press, 1933), p. 18.

5. Ibid. p. 1.

In other words, God is absolutely other. Man and God, time and eternity, are so qualitatively different that we are simply unable to speak of God. If we try, we find only ourselves speaking about ourselves (in a loud voice, as it were). This great gulf between God and us can be crossed only by God himself, and this he does in his word. Thus only in his revelation of himself can we know God.

In 1921 Barth was appointed to the chair of Reformed Theology at Göttingen, where his teaching duties forced him to do his own crash course in Reformed theology and history. And with this newfound knowledge of Calvin, Zwingli, the Reformed confessions and Schleiermacher he was beginning to amass a truly awesome theological arsenal with which he could wage war on liberalism.

Four years later he moved to teach at Münster, and in 1930 moved again: to Bonn. It was around that time that he was reading Anselm, and Anselm seemed to clarify things for him. From Anselm's maxim 'faith seeking understanding' he saw that theology must consist not of working things out by our own independent logic, but of thinking and understanding by faith, in the light of what God has said.[6]

In the 1950s the Swiss Roman Catholic theologian Hans Urs von Balthasar argued that around 1930 Barth's theology underwent an important change of direction: where previously Barth had argued for that dialectical relationship between God and man, from then he began to see that relationship as analogical (that there is in fact a correspondence ordained by God between God and humanity).[7] Barth himself (though aware of it) never disagreed with von Balthasar's theory, and thus the argument held sway for the decades to come. However, partly because of a major re-examination of that early stage of Barth's thinking by

---

6. Those who have read my introduction to Anselm in *The Breeze of the Centuries* (Nottingham: IVP, 2010) may notice that I have understood Anselm rather differently from the way Barth did.

7. H. U. von Balthasar, *The Theology of Karl Barth: Exposition and Interpretation* (San Fransisco: Ignatius, 1992).

Bruce McCormack,[8] and partly because of the recent publication of much previously unpublished material by Barth from the 1920s, that theory of a real change of direction now looks too crude. His 'dialectical' theology was not just a passing, immature phase. What happened around 1930 was a clarification: what Barth had more abstractly called 'the Word' was from then on quite clearly the specific person of Jesus Christ – who is the only way we can know God.

By the early 1930s, Barth had become Europe's leading Protestant thinker, and was ready to begin the project that would fill almost all of his remaining life: the writing of the *Church Dogmatics*. Yet no sooner had he started than Hitler came to power in Germany, changing everything. Much of German Protestantism swiftly bowed the knee; Barth, however, did not, seeing that capitulation as just the latest political expression of a theology derived from outside God's Word. For this he would soon lose his job. But it is what he did in the meantime that is most telling: quite apart from spearheading the creation of a confessing church that would resist accepting Nazi theology, Barth got down to the task of theology with even greater fervour. What Barth saw was that, instead of its being a time to abandon deep theology for quick response, now was the time to do theology all the more intensely in order to recover and safeguard the gospel.

As soon as he was dismissed from his teaching post in 1935, he was snapped up by Basel, and so found himself back in his native Switzerland. He did what he could to keep up pressure on the Nazis, but his time now was focused on the production of the *Church Dogmatics*.

The tough times, hard work and monumental reputation could easily lead one to miss something vital in Barth, and that is his Alp-climbing, pipe-loving sheer humanity. Endlessly curious and interested, he had a near mania for Mozart that was very revealing of him – Mozart surely appealed for how he shared Barth's own characteristic, twinkling, often impish, playfulness. And that,

---

8. B. McCormack, *Karl Barth's Critically Realistic Dialectical Theology: Its Genesis and Development, 1909–36* (Oxford: Oxford University Press, 1995).

Barth thought, was just how a theologian should be: 'The theologian who has no joy in his work is not a theologian at all. Sulky faces, morose thoughts and boring ways of speaking are intolerable.'[9]

In 1964 his health declined sharply, leaving him unable to work with anything like the ability he had had before. The end came in December 1968. He penned the words 'God is not a God of the dead but of the living' for a lecture he was due to give the next day, then folded his hands to pray. And that was how his wife, Nelly, found him – with, of course, Mozart playing in the background.

Church Dogmatics

The very title of Barth's magnum opus still shocks today. In direct and deliberate contrast to his nemesis, Schleiermacher, who wrote of the Christian's *faith* and experience, Barth wanted to write about absolute God-given truth – dogma.

After that, it is the gargantuan bulk and unfamiliar style that terrifies. Much of that fear can be quickly dispelled by coming to understand Barth's manner of writing (for the length of the work is really just a consequence of that manner). Barth believed that the task of theology is the same as the task of preaching, and thus preaching is just what he does in the *Church Dogmatics*. But preaching is not about merely conferring information: it is about winning hearts, and thus involves the sorts of persuasion and repetition that take time. Points must be reinforced, the readers won. The result is that Barth can be deeply moving to read. It also means he is peculiarly resistant to being quoted. Context is needed, and this is why, when he is quoted, he usually sounds impossibly complicated and so off-putting. Perhaps most important of all, though, the fact that Barth writes in such a sermonic, almost story-telling style actually means the reader can relax. Failing fully to grasp a few pages really will not matter, for the sweep of the argument is larger than that. Looking for the bigger picture is the main thing. Colin Gunton put it like this:

---

9. *Church Dogmatics* (Edinburgh: T. &. T Clark, 1956–75; hereafter *CD*) II/1,
    p. 656.

Barth is an aesthetic theologian. Barth worshipped before he theologized. His love for Mozart is to be noted here. The structure of Barth's theology is assertive, it is not argumentative; it can be considered as a sort of music. In the sense that Barth is not concerned to argue any more than Mozart is concerned to argue, Mozart just plays. I think that is Barth's aim: to play on the revelation of God so that its truth and beauty will shine.[10]

Of course, that does all mean that Barth demands you give him time. He will not dish out theological fast food. But giving him time does make one a more thoughtful theologian. Even in this little introduction, I hope, Barth should get you thinking and wondering, for agree or disagree with him (and you will almost certainly do both at different points), he is both stretching and stimulating. And as much as anything, that is probably because of another of his stylistic traits: he is deliberately (often infuriatingly) provocative.

Unfortunately, the mountainous proportions of the *Church Dogmatics* mean that this short sketch of them is going to have to be the most cartoon-like of all. Time dictates that we must fly past the intricacies of his argument and all those intriguing small print detours on everything from laughter to Leibniz. We must content ourselves with a bird's eye – no, satellite's eye – view.

There are four 'volumes' or main sections in the *Church Dogmatics*: *The Doctrine of the Word of God, The Doctrine of God, The Doctrine of Creation* and *The Doctrine of Reconciliation*. A fifth volume, *The Doctrine of Redemption* (on the Spirit and eschatology), was planned but never written (and Barth left no indication of what it would have looked like). In fact, even the fourth volume was cut short by Barth's death. Each 'volume' is divided up into part-volumes (each one an entire book), so that you have Volume I, part 1 (I/1), Volume III, part 2 (III/2) and so on.

Volume I: The Doctrine of the Word of God
I/1 In Barth's day, two practices had become conventional in writing complete works of theology like the *Dogmatics*. The first

---

10. C. E. Gunton, *The Barth Lectures* (London: T. &. T Clark, 2007), p. 63.

was to begin by asking if it is possible for God to be known.
Straightaway Barth disobeyed that rule, beginning his work by
arguing that the very question had things the wrong way round.
Why ask about some abstract possibility when God has actually
made himself known? The question, he believed, dangerously
overlooked what God has in fact done.

. The second convention was to do with the Trinity. Since
Schleiermacher had shunted the Trinity into an appendix at the
end of his *The Christian Faith*, it had become the most dust-covered
of all theological subjects. Again Barth rebelled and instead put the
Trinity at the very beginning of his theology, making it (and not
some general principle or view of God) the foundational presup-
position, the grammar for everything to follow.

What was even more revolutionary, though, was that Barth
combined the two subjects of revelation and Trinity. And thus his
theology begins with the God who makes himself known – that is,
the self-revealing Trinity. Because God is triune, he reveals himself
in a threefold word. First, there is Christ, the revealed word of
God; secondly, that revelation is attested to in the written word
of God, the Scriptures; and thirdly, those Scriptures are preached
or proclaimed, and so the world hears the one word of God.
However, it is not as if revelation is the mere giving of information; it is God himself coming to us, making himself known. God
the Father is the revealer; God the Son is the revelation; God the
Spirit is the 'revealedness', the one who enables us to perceive the
revelation.

Barth was seeking to apply the old Reformation banner of
'grace alone' to the doctrine of revelation. He wanted to reject all
Pelagianism in our knowledge of God (i.e. actually contributing to
it ourselves) to show that our knowledge of God is a divine gift,
unsupported by any presuppositions we may bring to it. Thus we
cannot decide in advance what God is like and then let his revelation simply add another storey to the structure we have made. We
cannot even know what 'God' truly means without revelation.
Thus Barth rejected all 'natural theology'.

He is commonly misunderstood here. He was not rejecting a
theology of creation, as we will go on to see; nor was he denying
that God speaks to us through creation: 'God may speak to

us through Russian Communism, a flute concerto, a blossom-
ing shrub, or a dead dog.'[11] The point was that we can come to
know God only in his Word; and once we have done that, we can
appreciate the true meaning of his revelation of himself elsewhere.
Natural theology proceeds in the opposite direction by first con-
structing its own theory of the possibility of knowing God, and
then using that as a yardstick by which to measure what may or
may not be true. In effect, it places the knowledge of God, and so
our faith, on a foundation other than God's revelation.

From revelation, Barth then goes on to focus on the triune
nature of this God. As Father, God reveals himself as the *creator*; as
Son he reveals himself as the *reconciler*; as Spirit he reveals himself
as the *redeemer*. Thus Barth shows his intent to have the very
structure of the *Dogmatics* shaped by the triune being of this God:
after looking at the doctrine of the word of God (vol. I) and the
doctrine of God as a whole (vol. II), his aim was to examine creation (vol. III, appropriated to the Father), reconciliation (vol. IV,
appropriated to the Son) and redemption (vol. V, appropriated to
the Spirit).

There was just one area of traditional trinitarian thought that,
he believed, needed to be re-expressed. The language of the three
'persons' of God he felt was misleading. God, he argued, is one
divine person or subject, not three; and, rather than speaking of
the three 'persons' of God, it would be more accurate to speak of
God existing in three 'ways of being'. This was not the old heresy
of modalism, he averred, and yet many today feel that he had at
least slipped in that direction.

I/2   The second part-volume on the word of God really serves
to flesh out that main theme of the triune God and his revelation
of himself. He begins with Jesus the revealed word of God, and
here we probably come closest to Barth's theological heartbeat. 'A
church dogmatics', he wrote, 'must, of course, be christologically
determined as a whole and in all its parts.'[12] Christ is the revelation
of God, and thus the Bible and all good theology must be about

11. *CD* I/1, p. 55.
12. *CD* I/2, p. 123.

pointing to and looking to him. Barth's favourite image (and one he had hung above his desk) was Grünewald's Isenheim altarpiece, where the prodigious pointing finger of John the Baptist directs viewers so clearly to the crucified Christ. For Barth, that summed up the task of the church and all its dogmatics.

From there he goes on to describe the Spirit as the one who enables us to receive the revelation of God. Under the heading of the Spirit, he then deals with Scripture, which, like the pointing finger, exists to bear witness to Christ, the revealed word of God. Barth never meant by this that Scripture is not itself the word of God. He scrupulously affirmed that.[13] His point was that the Bible is not an alternative way of knowing God next to Christ; it proclaims him.

Barth was so sensitive to the danger of studying the Scriptures without looking to Christ that he hit out hard against any tendency to raise the Bible to the place where Christ alone belongs. He would speak, for instance, of Scripture 'becoming', not 'being' the word of God to us. Fearful of the idea that we might view Scripture as a deposit of information that we now have at our disposal as the means by which we can work out our own knowledge of God, he preferred to speak of Scripture only becoming the word of God to us by God's grace through the Spirit. In other words, we never have the word of God at our disposal; we always depend on him in his grace to encounter us.

Even more strongly, for some of the same reasons he argued that, in the same way that Jesus, being human, had the potential within him for sin, so too the Scriptures, having human authors (as well as a divine author), have the potential to contain error. Those who hold to the infallibility of Scripture are surely right to be nervous about such statements, and our nerves are hardly helped by Barth's rhetoric here, when, for example, he speaks of Scripture's 'capacity for error'.[14] Yet while evangelicals have cause to be uncomfortable with some of Barth's formulations of biblical inspiration, it would be decidedly foolish simply to stop our ears

---

13. Ibid. 'Scripture as the Word of God', pp. 473–537.
14. Ibid. p. 509.

against him. The irony would be that we would leave ourselves deaf to one of Barth's most emphatic messages: that we submit all our thinking to Scripture as our absolute authority, as he himself always sought to do. Perhaps the way to get the most rounded understanding of Barth's view of Scripture is to see, not just what he says about it, but how he actually treats it in one of the many small-print exegetical sections of the *Dogmatics*. Of course one cannot expect to agree with his every point, but there one sees a theologian entirely shaped by the desire to hear and yield to Scripture.

From the word of God written he then moves to the word of God proclaimed. The church is to listen to the word of God and speak it. And this is where the practice of theology comes in: dogmatics summons the church to listen to the word of God afresh and so proclaim it faithfully.

Volume II: The Doctrine of God

II/1   By now readers need hardly be told that Barth will truck no belief in any 'God in general' unshaped by Jesus. Thus here now we will 'have to learn to say "God" in the correct sense'.[15] How? Not by asking 'What might or must God be like?' but by asking 'What has God actually shown himself to be like?' Everything to be said about knowledge of God really stems, for Barth, from the central fact that 'God is known only by God.'[16] That is, God knows himself in Christ, meaning that the sending of Christ was God's sharing of his own self-knowledge. But more: 'God is known *only* by God' and thus we can know God *only* in Christ.

What, then, do we learn about God from his revelation? Clearly, in Christ we see a God who seeks to create fellowship with us. Thus he is a God who loves. But God's revelation is truly revealing of who he is, and so it is not simply that God happens to love us, as if love could be some random blip in God. God has revealed himself to *be* a loving God. As Father, Son and Spirit, God is eternally loving without needing anything else to love. Furthermore,

---

15. *CD* II/1, p. 3.
16. Ibid. p. 179.

we do not see in Christ a God who needs to be in fellowship with us: we see in Christ a God who has life in himself, but who comes to share that life with us out of pure love. Thus we see a God who 'loves in freedom'. Unconstrained by anything, this God can be who he is: a freely loving God.

With that foundation in place Barth can examine what are traditionally called the divine attributes (though Barth prefers to call them divine 'perfections', 'attributes' suggesting that somehow we might have attributed these characteristics to God, instead of simply recognizing them in how he has revealed himself to be). Essentially, they are an unpacking of what it means for God to be 'the one who loves in freedom', and the result is a strikingly coherent picture. Instead of just giving a list of disconnected divine characteristics, Barth shows the interrelationship between God's perfections.

First, the perfections of God's love: we see God is gracious and holy, gracious in establishing fellowship with us, and holy in refusing to allow evil to remain as he seeks that fellowship. Similarly, he is merciful and righteous; he is also patient and wise, patient in even allowing his creatures to exist, and wise in so arranging things that they can.

Secondly, the perfections of God's freedom: God is one and omnipresent, constant and omnipotent, eternal and glorious. At first glance, this could look like a standard description of some 'God in general', but the actual content is quite specific. For example, instead of the traditional idea of God's immutability, which Barth feared could mean impersonal, abstract changelessness, he preferred to speak of God's constancy. And what, say, might omnipotence mean for this God?

> Jesus Christ the Crucified . . . is Himself the power of God. This is true in just the same sense as that the power of God is the power of His wisdom. It is in Him as the Crucified that all this is revealed and can be learned. The first lesson this teaches us is that we must really keep before our eyes God's reconciliation along with His revelation, that we must really understand His reconciliation itself as His revelation.[17]

---

17. Ibid. p. 607.

II/2 Next in the doctrine of God comes election. It comes here because Barth saw that election is essentially about God electing himself. He wanted to rid the doctrine of what he saw as the baleful influence of Augustine, who had taught a doctrine of election that seemed to have little to do with Christ.[18] Of course, the idea that what really underpins our salvation is some unknown divine decision and not Christ himself was intolerable for Barth. It not only pushed Christ aside; it suggested that God has not revealed his very self in Christ.

Instead, for Barth, there is no depth of God or salvation behind Christ; there is no decision in eternity other than him. Jesus Christ, then, is the one elected by God. And with Jesus' election, humanity in him is elected. Thus it is in Christ that God is gracious to humanity. In fact, not only is Christ the chosen one; on the cross he became the rejected one, taking on himself God's rejection of sinful humanity. Thus the only ones who remain rejected now are those who – perversely and against the truth – refuse the fact that God is for them.

Election for us, then, is being caught up into God's choice of Jesus Christ. But what should that relationship to which we have been called look like? It is to that question that Barth now turns. In choosing us, he says, God has freed us to choose him. God has been gracious and loving to us, freeing us to be gracious and loving. In other words, we have been freed by God to be Godlike. As God loves in freedom so we are freed to love (love of Christ being the only freedom).

Significantly, Barth strews all his ethics through the *Dogmatics* like this because he did not believe that ethics is a discipline that can be practised separately. Ethics can flow only directly from doctrine. Just as he shunned any doctrine that was abstracted from Christ, so he shunned any abstract ethics. So, for example, he would argue that the goodness of any action is determined by how Godlike (how gladly gracious) it is.

---

18. Barth preferred Athanasius here (and, in fact, more generally). Largely because he saw how profoundly shaped by Neoplatonism Augustine's theology was, he called it *süsses Gift* – 'sweet poison'!

Volume III: The Doctrine of Creation

III/1 There was much to recover in the doctrine of creation, Barth felt. Theologians had weakly allowed themselves to be pushed out of any serious study of creation by the natural scientists, meaning that the doctrine of creation had become a mere study of origins, losing what is specifically Christian about creation.

And creation is a specifically Christian doctrine, Barth held. It is an article of faith. God is a personal being, not merely an abstract principle that caused the world to be that any philosophy might be able to imagine. In fact, the creator is God the Father, and so the creator cannot be known other than through the Son. And it is not just the creator; the very creation itself can be understood only in the light of God's purposes revealed in Jesus Christ. That is because creation is all about the covenant relationship between God and humanity. Creation exists for the sake of that relationship. And that relationship is not therefore just a response to the Fall; it is the reason God created in the first place. Creation, therefore, simply cannot be understood without Christ, the one who brings about that relationship.

The act of creation happened when the internal goodness of God was turned outwards. The result is a creation that is itself good; not that that is self-evident, however (one could hardly conclude that by merely looking around us), but through revelation we learn the truth about creation: that it is good, and that light is stronger than darkness. And since creation is good, it can have a very real existence.

Note Barth's characteristically counter-intuitive logic in all this: we do not believe in a creator because we know about creation; rather, it is only because we know that God really exists that we can believe that creation really exists. Commenting on this, Colin Gunton observed that it is only under the influence of Christianity 'that the world has been affirmed in its full reality. In Platonism it isn't; in Hinduism it isn't – only where the Christian gospel has run have people believed that the world concretely exists.'[19]

III/2 Having argued that the relationship between God and

19. *Barth Lectures,* p. 252.

humanity is the reason for creation, Barth's next step is to look at humanity itself. Here we get to see how far Barth would carry his rejection of natural theology. Having argued that we are unable to know God without revelation, Barth now maintains that we are unable even to know what it is to be human without God revealing it to us! Only when we look at Jesus Christ can we know God's purposes for us, and so know who we are. 'Who and what man is, is no less specifically and emphatically declared by the Word of God than who and what God is.'[20]

In fact, Christ reveals to us what it is to be human because in a sense he is the first human. How? Because Christ shows that, in essence, 'to be a man is to be with God', and he is pre-eminently the one with God and the only one through whom any other can be with God.[21] It is not, though, that Christ is simply modelling to us what it is to be human; in Christ, man is with God and God with man. Thus sin, which is an attempt to be godless, is an attempt at the impossible – it is an 'impossible possibility'.[22]

Barth is strong in his use of such language, so strong that many have wondered if he is as a result promoting universalism, the idea that everyone will be saved. Barth repeatedly denied this, and yet even if the man himself did not want to go to that conclusion, the weight of a good deal of his theology certainly does seem to tip towards at least an extremely optimistic hope for all humanity.

III/3 Tying together the themes of the previous two part-volumes, Barth now examines how the creator is Lord over his creation. In other words, Barth looks at the doctrine of providence. Unsurprisingly, he wants an account of God's providence that is explicitly Christian. He is not interested in how, theoretically, a supreme being might relate to his creation; he wants to see specifically how this God acts.

God's lordship, he explains, is a fatherly lordship, and is expressed in the relationship between himself and Jesus Christ. His will for creation, and especially humanity, is really the outworking

---

20. *CD* III/2, p. 13.
21. Ibid. p. 135.
22. Ibid. p. 146.

of his will for Jesus Christ. His, then, is the most caring, preserving lordship!

So what of evil in creation? Barth defined evil as 'nothingness'. By that he was not even remotely implying that evil does not exist (having lived for so long in the shadow of Adolf Hitler, he was very aware of the reality of evil); it is that evil is what God has willed not to exist. God did not create it, and so it has no real being, but like a hole in the creation, it spoils what God has declared good and committed himself to. Like darkness, it is a lack that is and will be refuted and abolished by the shining of Christ, the Light of the world.

III/4 Barth finishes his account of creation with a look at what ethics flow from what has been seen. First, the ethics of creation cannot in any way be neutrally 'non-Christian' or generic. Far from it: 'the one command of the one God who is gracious to man in Jesus Christ is also the command of his Creator and therefore already the sanctification of the creaturely action and abstention of man'.[23] The Creator in his fatherly lordship calls humanity to himself, and that means our very existence is under command: to be human means we are called to confess and know him.

This has repercussions for the whole of life. Under the command of the Father, we are directed not only to him, but to each other. Our every relationship, from relations with our closest family to relations to those most distant from us are the outworkings of that basic obedience and enjoyment of him. And, since he affirms our existence, so too must we affirm our own lives 'and that of every other man as a loan, and to secure it against all caprice, in order that it may be used in this service and in preparation for this service'.[24] To be against life would mean being against the God who affirms it.

Volume IV: The Doctrine of Reconciliation
The fourth volume of the *Dogmatics* consists of three part-volumes (the third divided into two in the English translation: IV/3i and

23. *CD* III/4, p. 3.
24. Ibid. p. 324.

IV/3ii) and some posthumously published fragments of a fourth part-volume. The structure here is a little different: instead of being a sequential argument, this volume is more like a tapestry, with themes interwoven with each other. Doctrines that traditionally are kept separate (such as the person and the work of Christ) are here intertwined. This is because Barth was eager to show that it is wrong to divorce the person of Christ from what he came to do. What he does shows who he is; he is who he is in what he does.

Instead of arranging doctrines in some systematic order, Barth uses the volume to tell a story. The basic structure of that story is taken from the parable of the prodigal son. It starts with 'The Way of the Son of God into the Far Country' (not that the Son of God is wicked like the prodigal, but that he leaves his Father for a place that has become unclean), and it turns, triumphantly, into 'The Homecoming of the Son of Man'.

In order to appreciate what Barth is doing (and how elegantly he has arranged things), it is really necessary to read the three parts of 'The Doctrine of Reconciliation' alongside each other. The following table lays out how the various themes are picked up and treated in each part of Volume IV.

Part 1: Jesus Christ, the Lord as Servant	Part 2: Jesus Christ, the Servant as Lord	Part 3: Jesus Christ, the True Witness
§59 The Obedience of the Son of God	§64 The Exaltation of the Son of Man	§69 The Glory of the Mediator
§60 The Pride and Fall of Man	§65 The Sloth and Misery of Man	§70 The Falsehood and Condemnation of Man
§61 The Justification of Man	§66 The Sanctification of Man	§71 The Vocation of Man
§62 The Holy Spirit and the Gathering of the Christian Community	§67 The Holy Spirit and the Upbuilding of the Christian Community	§72 The Holy Spirit and the Sending of the Christian Community
§63 The Holy Spirit and Christian Faith	§68 The Holy Spirit and Christian Love	§73 The Holy Spirit and Christian Hope

IV/1 The first part tells the story of 'The Way of the Son of God into the Far Country', how Christ the Lord became a servant.

It concerns Jesus as God, coming to be God with us, humbling himself even to the cross. Typically, Barth reverses our expectations yet again: Jesus' humiliation and lowly servanthood are not associated with his humanity but with his divinity. And that reveals something infinitely profound about the very nature of God. It is that the humility of Jesus is not something strange and alien to God; the self-emptying of Jesus reveals that God's glory is his humble self-giving. That is what God in his lordship is like.

The lowest depth of the Son's obedient self-humbling was on the cross, when he became 'The Judge Judged in our Place'. There in our place he suffered under the death-dealing wrath that God's rejected love had become. And in so doing, he won a complete victory: 'The man of sin, the first Adam, the cosmos alienated from God, the "present evil world" (Gal. 1⁴), was taken and killed and buried in and with Him on the cross.'[25] The old humanity was destroyed so that he might be the new Adam of the real humanity God always intended.

True to form, Barth thought it quite impossible for us sinners to know naturally what sin is:

> Men preoccupied with themselves have no eyes to see this or categories to grasp it . . . Access to the knowledge that he is a sinner is lacking to man because he is a sinner . . . This is revealed in the fact that he does not see beyond the natural inward contradiction of his existence, in face of which he is capable of remorse and pity and melancholy, or even rueful irony, but not of genuine terror, in face of which he can always quieten and excuse himself, remaining obstinately blind and deaf to the contradiction which is his guilt and the breach which is his need. He sees and thinks and knows crookedly even in relation to his crookedness.[26]

It is only in Christ's judgment of sin (here especially on the cross) that sin is exposed and unmasked for what it is. And the divine humility of Jesus Christ here shows sin to be its rebellious polar

---

25. *CD* IV/1, p. 254.
26. Ibid. pp. 360–361.

opposite: it is pride. Reviling self-giving humility, I wish to be the lordly judge myself. Indeed:

> man only wants to judge. He thinks he sits on a high throne, but in reality he sits only on a child's stool, blowing his little trumpet, cracking his little whip, pointing with frightful seriousness his little finger, while all the time nothing happens that really matters. He can only play the judge. He is only a dilettante, a blunderer . . .[27]

But then, Christ is the answer to that, too. Not only was he judged in our place, but he is the judge in our place; meaning we can abandon our silly conceit.

Throughout his whole doctrine of reconciliation, Barth weaves the traditional designation of Christ as prophet, priest and king. Here Christ is seen to be our priest, achieving reconciliation between God and humanity, and in particular, achieving our justification.

Then, finally, he looks at the Holy Spirit's role in forming the body of Christ, the church, the gathering of those he makes willing through faith to live under God's condemnation of the proud old humanity.

IV/2 The story now does a U-turn as we see 'The Homecoming of the Son of Man' and Jesus Christ the servant's being Lord. It describes Jesus as the man (the new and true man) who is exalted to be with God in his resurrection and ascension. And, as his humility was associated with his divinity, now his humanity is associated with his exaltation. Jesus is now depicted as the Son of Man in his kingly office, enthroned by God. In him, man is now with God and we see what we are meant to be as human.

This exaltation further exposes sin as the sloth that miserably refuses to join Jesus as he goes to his Father. In the resurrection of the Son of Man, then, we see his (defeated) antithesis:

> the man who would not make use of his freedom, but was content with the low level of a self-enclosed being, thus being irremediably and

---

27. Ibid. p. 446.

radically and totally subject to his own stupidity, inhumanity, dissipation and anxiety, and delivered up to his own death.[28]

However, in his resurrection and ascension, Jesus has brought man to be with God, and so made it possible for us to reject our sloth and be sanctified. In establishing what it is to be truly human, truly alive and with God, he frees us from our pretentiousness to be for God and for our fellow man. Liberated to be truly human, we are thus liberated to be Godlike, loving.

Finally, Barth turns to look at how the Spirit builds up the body of Christ into the maturity of Godlike love. So empowered, the church can then represent to the world the freedom and humanity Christ has brought.

IV/3 The third part deals with Christ as prophet. By that, Barth does not mean that Christ is about proclaiming some message other than himself: unlike all other prophets, in everything he does he announces himself as the mediator, the one who unites God and humanity in himself. 'Revelation takes place in and with reconciliation. Indeed, the latter is also revelation. As God acts in it, He also speaks. Reconciliation is not a dark or dumb event, but perspicuous and vocal.'[29] Barth's preferred image here is of the light of life: Christ's life-giving reconciliation is light-giving.

This light of truth exposes sin as a perverse self-condemning lie, an attempt to hide from the truth of Christ and grasp life on man's own, sinful terms. But Christ calls and awakens us to know the truth and then proclaim that truth to the world. He therefore gives us his enlightening Spirit to overcome the deceit in us, to cause us to hope in him and call all people to know that hope.

IV/4 A fourth part, which Barth never lived to complete, would have looked at our faith-response to this reconciliation, and how, as we are baptized with the Spirit, we are called to be baptized with water as the 'first step of this life of faithfulness to God'.[30]

---

28. *CD* IV/2, p. 378.
29. *CD* IV/3i, p. 8.
30. *CD* IV/4, p. 2.

Going on with Barth

There is no end of books, articles and websites on Barth. Yet there is really very little that is genuinely accessible and helpful for the beginner, and all the 'Barth-speak' can feel like razor wire designed to keep out the uninitiated. A couple of books stand out as good next steps, though: for an overwhelmingly positive introduction and assessment, try John Webster's *Karl Barth* (London: Continuum, 2000); or, for a delightful and more critical review, get Colin Gunton's *The Barth Lectures* (London: T. & T. Clark, 2007). The latter will also give you the joy of getting to know the late, great Colin Gunton and some of his theology.

But by now, readers should not be surprised that I recommend going straight to read the man himself. Armed with the knowledge of his narrative style, you can. Really you can jump into the *Church Dogmatics* wherever appeals, but many find little III/1 a good place for a first visit. Or, if the *Dogmatics* still just seems too much, go for his short *Evangelical Theology: An Introduction* (Grand Rapids: Eerdmans, 2004), or perhaps his *Dogmatics in Outline* (London: SCM, 1949).

Karl Barth timeline

1886	Barth born in Basel
1904	Theological studies in Berne, Berlin, Tübingen and Marburg
1909	Assistant pastor in Geneva
1911	Pastor in Safenwil
1914	Barth's liberal teachers endorse the First World War
1916	Studies Romans
1919	Commentary on Romans published
1921	Professor of Reformed Theology in Göttingen
1925	Lecturer in Münster
1930	Professor of Systematic Theology in Bonn; begins writing *Church Dogmatics*
1933	Adolf Hitler becomes Chancellor of Germany
1934	Co-authors the Barmen Declaration for the Confessing Church in Germany, rejecting Nazi theology; writes *No!* against Emil Brunner's openness to natural theology
1935	Dismissed from his teaching post and appointed Professor of Theology in Basel
1939–45	Second World War
1940	Volunteers for the Swiss Army
1962	Retires from professorship
1968	Barth dies

BACK TO THE SOURCES!

The lovely landscape of thirteenth-century Italy was studded up and down with ancient and crumbling remains. It was hard to miss the fact that here had once been a glorious and imperial civilization. In practice, though, all those arches, pillars and heaps of marble blocks were seen to be useful only as free quarries: the stone could be taken and used for new building projects, the marble turned into agricultural lime and spread round farms. Unappreciated for what it was, the past was being raped.

Then somehow the mood changed and people began instead to look more to that classical past for inspiration. 'Back to the sources!' was the new cry. And with that, there was an explosion of creativity. There was Renaissance. Rebirth. Under the influence of a rediscovered past, the worlds of art, literature, science, philosophy (and soon, theology) were seized with freshness and energy. Even the new buildings looked quite different; not because more stone was being pilfered from old ruins, but because now the very style of classical architecture was inspiring a taste for beautiful proportion and clean lines.

The refreshment of the past

Of course, it is quite possible to revel in the past in such a way as to become a reactionary or a romantic. But the Renaissance shows that we can also be refreshed by it. In fact, is that not what roots are for? The healthiest trees in a forest are those with the most extensive roots, for it is by using their roots that trees thrive and blossom. If a tree is to grow great, its roots must go deep. It is when those roots are cut that they die. It is no different in the church: without good roots into the past, we will be blown around by the assumptions of our generation, overly sensitive to petty changes in our immediate environment, ever more pinched and puny, our gospel all puckered and sour. But simply try this experiment at home: trot out some insight from Edwards or Athanasius, don't name your source, and people will think you dazzlingly original and fresh. Worrying? Maybe. But clearly, what is old can be new.

Go on!

That, at least, has been the aim of this utterly unoriginal book: to explore and appreciate roots, to sense some of the refreshment (and challenge) available. Has it worked? It has certainly been but a tiny effort, and for all the inclusion of some theologians, the necessary constraints of space have sadly meant the exclusion of so many. Oh to have spent time with others, perhaps feisty Tertullian or Bernard of Clairvaux. But my real fear now is that readers will go away with the wrong idea. Reading the greats ought to breed modesty, and he who spends time with these giants should sense what a clod he is. The reality, though, is that even the vaguest familiarity with a celebrity can induce the most cockeyed egotism. Thus if somehow I have left any reader feeling that he is a match for even one of these theologians, I apologize now. The attempt to introduce simply can convey the impression that the subjects are simple. But to have mastered an introduction to a theologian is not to have mastered a theologian.

That is why this is not a conclusion, for the whole point of this book has been, not to bag and collect, but to introduce, to lead on. And if you have managed to wade this far through the introductions, then getting to know the men themselves will be a delight. Great theologians are usually infinitely more interesting than the things said about them. So go on: back to the sources!

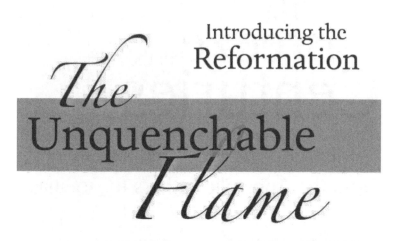
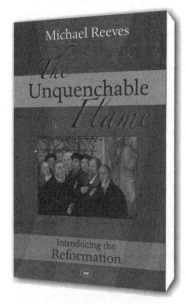

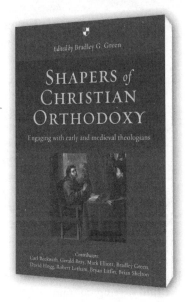

related titles from Apollos

Engaging with Barth
Contemporary evangelical critiques

ISBN: 978-1-84474-245-5

This collection of essays engages critically and courteously with Karl Barth on a range of topics where, for the contributors, his interpretation of Scripture, reading of church history, and confession of Christian doctrine are unsatisfactory.

This engagement is offered as a positive contribution to the wider programme of constructive theological reflection that seeks to articulate the gospel of Jesus Christ in and for the contemporary world.

Engaging with Calvin
Aspects of the Reformer's legacy for today

ISBN: 978-1-84474-398-8

Five hundred years after his birth, the ideas of John Calvin continue to influence churches all around the world.

These essays explore selected aspects of Calvin's contribution and encourage us to read Calvin for ourselves – because to engage with him as he speaks about the knowledge of God the Creator and Redeemer, whom he served with a singular devotion, cannot but mean that we will have our vision of God expanded and our love for him inflamed.